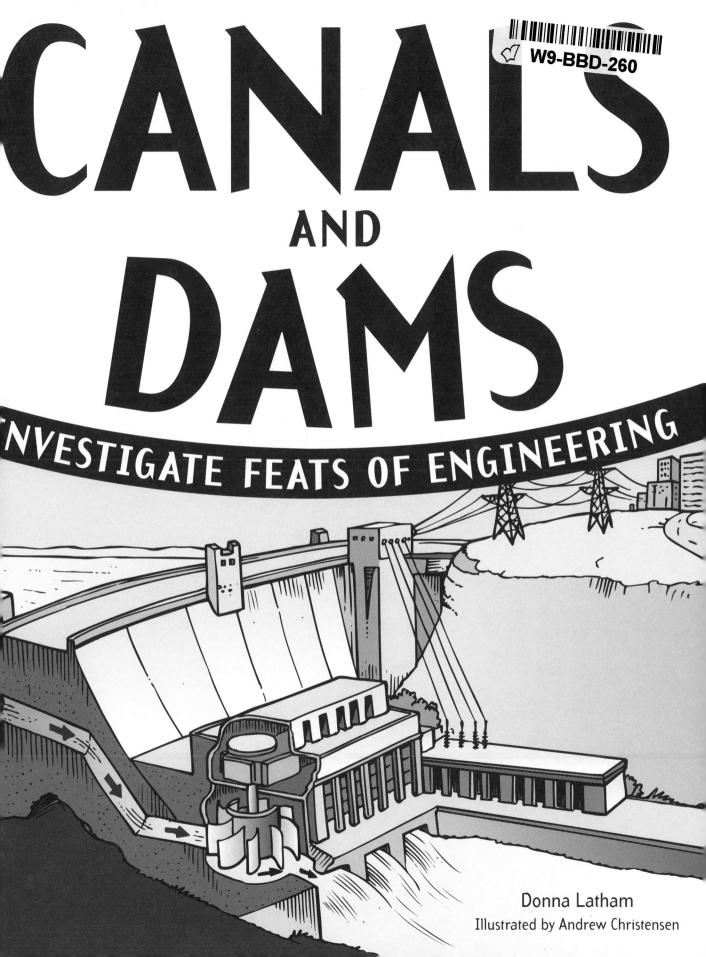

CANALS
AND
DAMS

INVESTIGATE FEATS OF ENGINEERING

Donna Latham

Illustrated by Andrew Christensen

Nomad Press
A division of Nomad Communications
10 9 8 7 6 5 4

Softcover ISBN: 978-1-61930-165-8
Hardcover ISBN: 978-1-61930-169-6

Illustrations by Andrew Christensen
Educational Consultant, Marla Conn

Questions regarding the ordering of this book should be addressed to
Nomad Press
2456 Christian St.
White River Junction, VT 05001
www.nomadpress.net

CONTENTS

For Robbie Borland and Arden Esvang.
Builders of the future.

Sincere thanks to hydrologist and cheerleader extraordinaire Nick Longo and to physicist Eric Prebys, Ph.D, at Fermilab in Batavia, Illinois.

More engineering titles in the *Build It Yourself* Series

3100 BCE OR EARLIER: Ancient Greek engineers develop flat-bottomed basins with simple sluice gates to capture Nile River floodwaters for irrigation.

2700 BCE: Ancient Egyptians construct Sadd-el-Kafara Dam, one of the world's earliest dams, along the Nile River. When floodwaters wipe out the embankment dam, engineers give up on the idea of damming.

1200 BCE: Ancient engineers build Las Capas, the earliest irrigation system in America. The system routes water from the Santa Cruz River to the Sonoran Desert and allows hunter-gatherers to begin farming.

19 BCE: Ancient Roman engineers develop hydraulic concrete using volcanic ash. It allows them to build underwater structures. Some are still preserved today.

1500 CE: In Venice, Italy, the artist, inventor, and scientist Leonardo da Vinci gains inspiration from canals and waterways. He explores principles of buoyancy.

1825: The Erie Canal opens, linking Lake Erie with the Atlantic Ocean.

1869: Egypt's Suez Canal is completed, linking the Red Sea and the Mediterranean Sea. The canal saves ships 6,000 miles of travel (9,656 kilometers) around Africa.

1899: Pounding rains and snowmelt smash Johnstown, Pennsylvania, causing the South Fork Dam to fail. A wall of 20 million tons of water devastates the community, killing over 2,200 people.

1914: The Panama Canal opens. The international waterway links the Atlantic and Pacific Oceans, saving 8,000 miles of travel (over 12,000 kilometers) around South America.

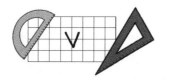

1936: The Hoover Dam is built to control the Colorado River. Workers toil in hazardous conditions and sizzling heat on the border of Nevada and Arizona.

1943: During World War II, British pilots destroy Nazi Germany's hydroelectric dams with "bouncing bombs."

1963: Vajont Dam in the Italian Alps fails, and a disastrous landslide overwhelms the area.

1970: Aswan High Dam along the Nile River in Aswan, Egypt, is completed. The dam is praised as the twentieth century's greatest feat of engineering.

1978: Chemicals dumped in the Love Canal near Niagara Falls, New York, harm people and the environment. It is one of the most notorious environmental tragedies in the United States.

2005: Hurricane Katrina slams southeastern Louisiana and floods New Orleans in a devastating disaster.

2006: Three Gorges Dam, over China's Yangtze River, is completed. The world's largest hydroelectric project displaces over a million people and destroys the Yangtze River dolphin's habitat.

2008: Truckee Canal fails because of damage from rodents, releasing frigid water that floods Fernley, Nevada.

2012: Hurricane Isaac slams New Orleans and the Gulf Coast on the anniversary of Hurricane Katrina. The fortified levees hold.

2012: Record drought in the midwestern United States radically reduces water levels in Indiana's Salamonie River. A town submerged for dam construction in 1965 rises up.

2012: Melting Arctic ice opens Arctic waters. It raises critical questions about new global trade routes and future water control.

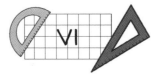

WATER TAMERS

HOW DO YOU START YOUR MORNINGS?

Maybe you take a shower. After breakfast, do you brush your teeth and rinse your mouth? Do you wash your dishes? All of this requires water. Our blue planet is a watery place, with water covering about 70 percent of its surface. In fact, there's so much water it's easy to take it for granted. We twist a tap or a spigot. Presto! Flowing water. Water is an important **natural resource**, but where does it come from? The answer might surprise you.

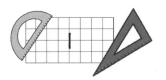

But there is really nothing natural about the way we get our water.

WORDS to KNOW

natural resource: a material or substance such as gold, wood, and water that occurs in nature and is valuable to humans.

dam: a barrier built across a river or stream to control and collect water.

reservoir: an artificial lake or tank for collecting and storing water.

hydroelectricity: electricity generated from water power.

levee: a wall of earth or stone built along a riverbank to prevent flooding of the land.

canal: a man-made waterway built for shipping, navigation, or **irrigation**.

irrigation: supplying land with water using pipes and ditches, usually for crops.

freshwater: water that is not salty.

People build **dams** across rivers. These dams create **reservoirs** to store water supplies and produce **hydroelectricity**. People also build **levees** and **canals** to channel water to homes and fields and keep rivers running where we want them to go.

Why do people control water in these ways when there is so much water on Earth? Because there's a lot of water in some areas, while other areas are too dry.

Across the planet, man-made systems move water from deeper river basins to drier river basins. And we're talking about huge amounts of water going huge distances. The California State Water Project, for example, moves 6.6 billion gallons (25 billion liters) each year over a distance of 444 miles (715 kilometers)! In fact, so much **freshwater** moves from river basin to river basin every year in the United States, it's like moving 22 Colorado Rivers!

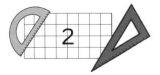

2

DID YOU KNOW?

The Colorado River is the United States' fifth-largest river! Its **course** flows 1,450 miles from its source in the Rocky Mountains to its mouth at the Gulf of California in Mexico's Sonoran Desert (2,330 kilometers).

Water sustains life. As long as people have lived on Earth, they've depended on freshwater for survival. Long ago, hunter-gatherers followed wild animals to hunt as the seasons changed. They gathered fruits and seeds and searched for freshwater wherever they went.

Sometime about 10,000 years ago, people started settling down in one place and growing their own

WORDS to KNOW

course: the path a river takes from its source, where it begins, to its mouth, where it empties.

crop: a plant grown for food and other uses.

ancestors: the people that lived before you.

crops. What do crops need? Sun, of course, but also water! As populations grew and the best land near water sources was taken, people had to settle farther and farther away from springs and rivers. This created an enormous problem for farming. Our **ancestors** needed to move water supplies from one place to another.

TRY THIS

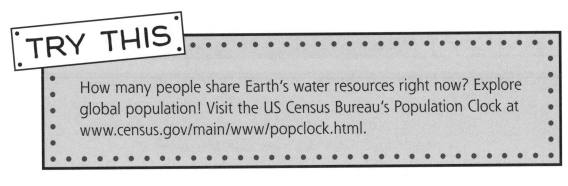

How many people share Earth's water resources right now? Explore global population! Visit the US Census Bureau's Population Clock at www.census.gov/main/www/popclock.html.

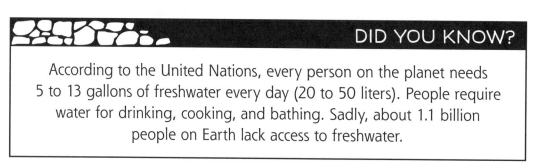

What was the **solution**? How could people move water from mountain streams to villages? And how could they store the water so it was available when it was needed? By thinking big and building big, people tackled these challenges.

Waterways are lifelines. Over the ages, people designed inventive methods to transfer and store water. They relied on engineering.

Canals and dams are water tamers that change a river's natural flow of water. These incredible feats of engineering are symbols of human **ingenuity** and **innovation**.

DID YOU KNOW?

According to the United Nations, every person on the planet needs 5 to 13 gallons of freshwater every day (20 to 50 liters). People require water for drinking, cooking, and bathing. Sadly, about 1.1 billion people on Earth lack access to freshwater.

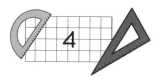

Throughout human history, **engineers** have worked to improve life for themselves and others. Early engineers observed the way nature worked and teamed with it to make all kinds of improvements. It wasn't always easy, and engineers made monumental mistakes along the way. Still, they remained determined. They explored ways to design tools, machines, and **structures**.

Engineers make our modern world possible.

WATER POWER

Water has been **pivotal** in world history. People toiled to harness waterpower as they built cities, raised crops, and transported goods. They filled in waterlogged areas like swamps and marshes, and worked to hold back destructive floodwaters.

WORDS to KNOW

engineer: someone who uses science and math to design and build structures such as buildings, bridges, **tunnels**, canals, and dams.

tunnel: a passageway that goes through or under natural or man-made obstacles such as rivers, mountains, roads, and buildings.

structure: a bridge, tunnel, building, dam, or other object built from a number of different parts put together in a certain way.

pivotal: vitally important.

Countries have even gone to war over water. In *Water: The Epic Struggle for Wealth, Power, and Civilization*, Steven Solomon writes, "Today, there is hardly an accessible freshwater resource on the planet that is not being engineered, often monumentally, by man."

Notable Quotable

"Anyone who has never made a mistake never tried anything new."
—Albert Einstein (1879–1955), physicist and winner of the Nobel Prize

THE DAWN OF ENGINEERING

As long as there have been people, there have been engineers. Over 72,000 years ago, early humans in South Africa used fires for cooking, heat, and light. Ancient engineers discovered that flames improved cutting edges on tools. At Pinnacle Post on South Africa's coast, researchers discovered stone tools made from silcrete. But silcrete is a crumbly rock that can fall apart in the chipping process that early toolmakers used. These tools were a deep, glossy red, different from the brown silcrete at the site.

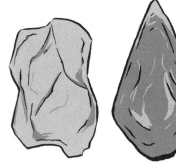

It turns out that the tools weren't chiseled at all—they were **pyroengineered**! Heating the silcrete made it **brittle** so it was easier to break in clean lines. These tools had such sharp edges they sliced animal skins like a razor blade!

Archaeologist Kyle Brown **theorized** that early modern humans buried silcrete stones under a huge fire. Brown tested his theory by burning stones for 10 hours. When the rocks cooled, they had a reddish shine and were hardened. Because the cooling prevented cracking and shattering, the stones made excellent material for precise tools. Tens of thousands of years later, we still use heat treatment to change many materials. Have you ever heard about melting sand to make glass?

WORDS to KNOW

pyroengineer: to use fire in toolmaking to treat stones.

brittle: easily broken, cracked, or snapped.

archaeologist: a scientist who studies ancient people through the objects left behind.

theorize: to come up with an idea that explains how or why something happens.

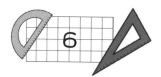

Notable Quotable

"Heating stones is the dawn of human engineering. One of the things that makes us uniquely human is that we can take things in our landscape and adapt them. We engineer them to fit our needs."

—*Kyle Brown, archaeologist*

People built early canals and dams long before the study of **physics**. But they still used astonishing scientific and mathematical know-how. Over thousands of years, they experimented with **trial and error**. In search of knowledge and with a spirit of generosity, people shared their discoveries. The **technological** advances enabled people to master the **principles** of building big. Engineers risked their lives to advance our world with waterpower. Using natural resources, man-made materials, and the **forces** of nature, engineers developed ways to tame water.

WORDS to KNOW

physics: the science of how **matter** and **energy** work together. A physicist studies physics.

matter: what an object is made of.

energy: the ability to do work.

trial and error: trying first one thing, then another and another, until something works.

technological: a way of applying tools and methods to do something.

principle: the basic way that something works.

force: a push or pull that changes an object's motion.

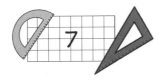

7

Building a huge structure like a canal or dam comes with benefits and risks.

People were often **displaced** to make way for structures that brought water and power to millions. **Habitats** were destroyed.

While trying to improve lives, people literally changed the face of the planet. But at what cost? Engineers didn't always consider the impact on the **environment**. They often underestimated the forces of nature.

WORDS to KNOW

displace: to force people, animals, or things from their usual place.

habitat: the natural area where a plant or an animal lives.

environment: everything in nature, living and nonliving, including plants, animals, soil, rocks, and water.

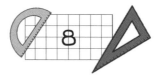

Notable Quotable

"The Mississippi River will always have its own way.
No engineering skill can persuade it to do otherwise."
—Mark Twain (1835–1910), American author and steamboat pilot

When canals **collapsed** or dams were **breached**, water's life-sustaining powers could turn deadly. Devastating floods swallowed crops, drowned **livestock**, and wiped out whole communities.

People wondered, are we really in control? What happens when we change the environment? Can we conquer nature? Can we ever truly tame water?

WORDS to KNOW

collapse: to fall in or down suddenly.

breach: to make an opening through something.

livestock: animals raised for food or other products.

ABOUT THE PROJECTS

Keep reading! Build the projects in this book to learn how canals and dams are built. See what happens when they succeed and when they fail. Most of the projects in this book involve items you might have around the house. Remember that safety's first, so ask adults for help around water and when handling pins, nails, screwdrivers, and other sharp objects.

Use the activities to make your own discoveries about canals and dams and other engineering marvels. Along the way you'll explore the engineering process. Let your ideas and ingenuity spark your own innovations.

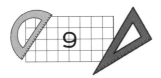

ENGINEERING AND THINKING BIG

YOU PROBABLY DON'T REALIZE HOW FASCINATING
the engineering profession really is. Engineers use science
and math, but they also use experience, judgment, and
common sense to make things that are useful and benefit
our lives in countless ways. They come up with creative
and practical solutions to **technical** problems.

10

Engineers design and build structures, machines, and systems. They create amazing products that are safe and reliable and that we use all the time. Using properties of light, engineers develop fiber optic gloves that shine fingertip spotlights. Applying principles of **chemistry**, engineers have improved antibiotics for infected toenails. They make a difference in your everyday life and you don't even realize it.

WORDS to KNOW

technical: relating to scientific or mechanical methods.

chemistry: the science of how substances interact, combine, and change.

stealth: silent or secret.

DID YOU KNOW?

Nearly everything we use and depend on has been engineered. This includes everything from kitchen gizmos like onion goggles and soda-fizzers to palm-sized e-readers, featherweight bike frames, and energy-efficient cars. Engineers develop smart stethoscopes that help medical students recognize abnormal heartbeats. They design retainers that hold your teeth in place once you get your braces off. But engineering is called "the **stealth** profession." That's because engineers work behind the scenes. We hardly ever hear about the talented but "invisible" engineers who devise many of the creations on which we all rely.

BRANCHES OF ENGINEERING

Engineers hold about 1.6 million jobs in the United States. The field of engineering is constantly changing, but it includes five major branches: chemical, civil, computer, electrical, and mechanical.

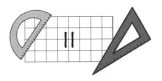

BRANCHES OF ENGINEERING

CHEMICAL	Using science to convert raw materials and chemicals into things people can use, such as food and energy products.
CIVIL	Designing and building bridges, buildings, dams, highways, and tunnels.
COMPUTER	Designing technology, such as computer software and hardware, operating systems, and computer networks.
ELECTRICAL	Designing electrical systems and electronic products.
MECHANICAL	Designing mechanical systems, such as engines, tools, and machines.

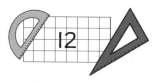

THE ENGINEERING DESIGN PROCESS

Engineering is a group effort. It allows for the open exchange of ideas. The Engineering Design Process is a series of steps engineers follow when they tackle a problem. These steps lead to a solution, which is often a new product, system, or structure. Specific steps in the process might vary, but they typically involve identifying a problem, brainstorming, designing, building a **prototype**, testing, evaluating, and redesigning.

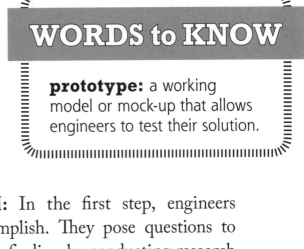

WORDS to KNOW

prototype: a working model or mock-up that allows engineers to test their solution.

IDENTIFY THE PROBLEM: In the first step, engineers figure out what they need to accomplish. They pose questions to target their goal. They engage in fact-finding by conducting research and collecting information.

BRAINSTORM SOLUTIONS: Now, engineers let their ideas fly like lightning. In a group, they share creative and sudden ideas, no matter how "impossible" they may seem. One clever idea can spark unexpected solutions or methods. After brainstorming, engineers sort the ideas to target the most likely solution and focus on it.

DESIGN AND DRAW A PLAN: At this step, engineers draw a diagram of the solution to their problem. They note which tools and building materials are required to proceed.

BUILD A PROTOTYPE: A prototype is an important component of testing and research. It allows engineers to notice a missing piece they may have overlooked. Others can share their ideas for improvement or see something that might not work.

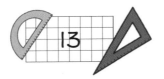

TEST THE PROTOTYPE: As a team, engineers conduct tests. They observe how the prototype measures up to the design.

EVALUATE THE OUTCOME: At this step, engineers discuss what worked or didn't work with the design. They share ideas for improvements in design or materials.

REDESIGN WITH IMPROVEMENTS: Engineers apply suggestions for improvement and develop a stronger product to test.

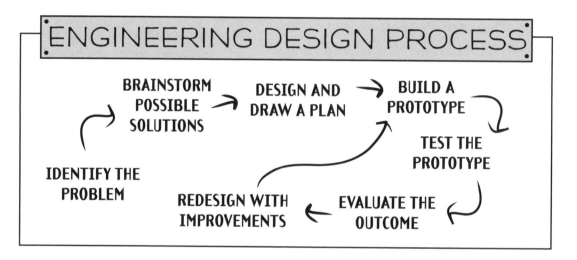

ENGINEERING DESIGN PROCESS

BRAINSTORM POSSIBLE SOLUTIONS → DESIGN AND DRAW A PLAN → BUILD A PROTOTYPE → TEST THE PROTOTYPE → EVALUATE THE OUTCOME → REDESIGN WITH IMPROVEMENTS → IDENTIFY THE PROBLEM

Do you notice how the Engineering Design Process flow chart connects the steps with arrows? That keeps the design process **open-ended** so the engineers can adapt to the needs of the situation. Engineers might have to throw out one idea and come up a new solution. They might double back to revisit a step or two. An earlier idea that was rejected might turn out to be promising. Frequently, several solutions are possible, so engineers devise multiple solutions.

WORDS to KNOW

open-ended: able to adapt to the needs of a situation.

14

CIVIL ENGINEERING

Civil engineering is called the "mother of all engineering disciplines." It's considered the oldest branch, the one that gave birth to all the others. Civil engineers design, construct, and maintain bridges, buildings, canals, dams, highways, and tunnels. They confront problems by asking questions such as: How can we build a canal that won't destroy ancient structures? How do we alter water's north to south flow? How can we design a dam to withstand **earthquakes** and **landslides**?

WORDS to KNOW

earthquake: a sudden movement in pieces of the outer layer of the earth.

landslide: the sliding down of a mass of earth or rock from a mountain or cliff.

interaction: how things work together.

load: an applied force or weight.

FORCES: PUSHES AND PULLS

Physics is a branch of science that deals with the physical world. It centers on matter and energy and their **interactions**. Engineers apply principals of physics to build structures that resist forces. A force is a push or pull.

PUSH

PULL

Forces make things move or change position. The forces that are exerted on big structures like canals and dams are called **loads**. If structures aren't able to withstand forces, they split apart and collapse.

What's one force that is always pulling on canals and dams, and you? **Gravity**. Gravity is an invisible force that's acting on you right now. It's constantly pulling you and everything on Earth toward the earth's center. Engineers know that the canals and dams they build must withstand the natural force of gravity so they don't collapse.

WORDS to KNOW

gravity: a physical force that pulls bodies toward the center of the earth.

tsunami: an enormous wave formed by a disturbance under the water, like an earthquake or volcano.

hydraulic engineering: water control and transportation.

channel: a long narrow passage or tube along which a liquid can flow.

Canals and dams must resist other environmental forces.

They must stand up to **tsunamis** that slam them and violent earthquakes that shove them from side to side. Unfortunately, musts don't always work out. Collapse is a reality for both canals and dams, and when this happens, flooding impacts people, animals, and the environment.

DID YOU KNOW?

Hydraulic engineering is an area of civil engineering. Hydraulic engineers work with fluid flow and transportation. They design canals, **channels**, dams, and levees.

GET A LOAD OF THESE!

Engineers rely on knowledge of **statics** to build structures. They have to understand forces and the ways they produce **equilibrium**.

To remain static, structures must withstand forces and loads. Loads of loads! A structure must be able to support its own weight. This is its **dead load**.

A dam's dead load includes its enormous concrete base and immense steel pipes. It includes every pin, rivet, and nail holding the pipes in place. Every bit of grout used to connect joints adds to the load. In a structure such as a building, the dead load includes all the furniture, machines, and equipment inside.

Engineers also have to consider **live loads**. These are the people and vehicles acting on a structure. Inside a house or school, you're part of the live load. A dam's live load might be a reservoir built to collect and store water.

WORDS to KNOW

statics: an area of physics related to forces and the ways they produce equilibrium.

equilibrium: the state of balance between opposing forces.

dead load: the actual, constant weight of a structure.

live load: the changing weight of vehicles, pedestrians, and other things that are placed on a structure.

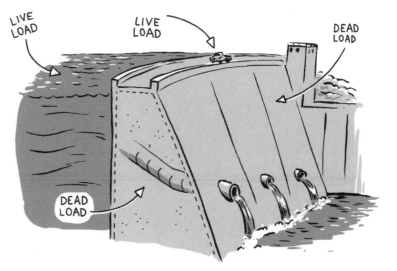

LIVE LOAD

LIVE LOAD

DEAD LOAD

DEAD LOAD

Loads don't always stay the same. **Dynamic loads** change. They're applied to structures through motion. What dynamic loads impact structures? Ferocious winds, pounding waters, and rattling earthquakes clobber structures of all sizes, from tiny houses to mammoth dams.

UNDER PRESSURE

To design and construct canals and dams, **pressure** is another force for engineers to consider. Both of these structures must resist the pushing force of **water pressure**. Water constantly pushes against canals and dams. Have you ever gone to the bottom of a deep pool? Maybe you've noticed that the water seemed to press against you. Your ears might have ached and popped. That's because your eardrums experienced intensified pressure!

The deeper you go, the more the pressure increases. The deeper a body of water is, the greater its pressure. For example, a diver taking photos 40 feet underwater (12 meters), will experience twice the pressure another diver feels at 20 feet deep (6 meters).

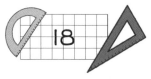

Notable Quotable
"Imagination decides everything."
—*Blaise Pascal, physicist and inventor of the syringe,* **hydraulic press***, and more.*

Pascal's Law is a concept of **physical science** that engineers of canals and dams use. Blaise Pascal (1623–1662) was a French physicist, inventor, and mathematician. He shared major ideas and observations about **fluids**. His law states that pressure placed on a fluid inside a container spreads equally in all directions. Pressure spreads throughout the container and stays constant.

WORDS to KNOW

hydraulic press: a machine that uses liquid pressure to exert force on a small piston, which moves a larger piston.

physical science: the study of the physical world.

fluid: a substance such as a gas or a liquid that flows freely and has no fixed shape.

TRY THIS

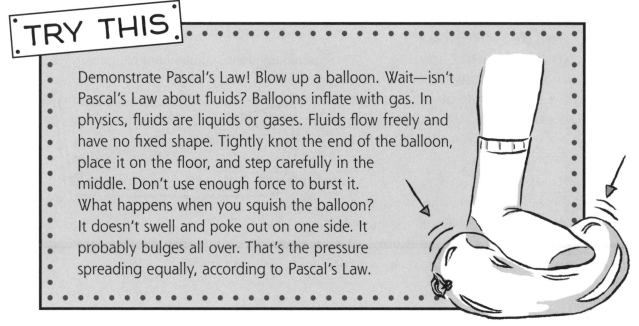

Demonstrate Pascal's Law! Blow up a balloon. Wait—isn't Pascal's Law about fluids? Balloons inflate with gas. In physics, fluids are liquids or gases. Fluids flow freely and have no fixed shape. Tightly knot the end of the balloon, place it on the floor, and step carefully in the middle. Don't use enough force to burst it. What happens when you squish the balloon? It doesn't swell and poke out on one side. It probably bulges all over. That's the pressure spreading equally, according to Pascal's Law.

Watershed in a Tub

SUPPLIES: *aquarium gravel, large plastic tub, 2 pounds modeling clay (0.9 kilogram), 3 pounds sand (1½ kilograms), medium-sized plastic tub, paint stirrer, bucket of water, aluminum foil, spray bottle of water, ¼ cup powdered cocoa (57 grams)*

Early **civilizations** sprang up along water sources. A watershed is a land area that drains into a stream, lake, river, or ocean.

HINT: You can swap any waterproof material, such as wax paper or plastic wrap, for aluminum foil.

WORDS to KNOW

civilization: a community of people that is advanced in art, science, and government.

aquifer: a layer of sand, gravel, and rock that has pores or openings through which groundwater flows.

groundwater: water located in the ground.

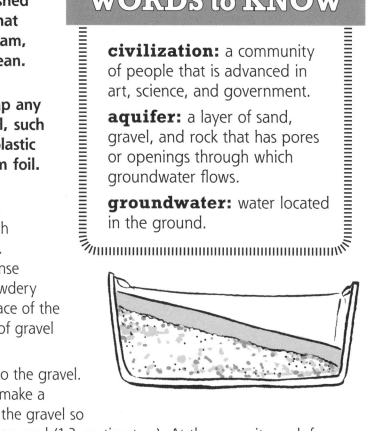

1 Gravel represents the **aquifer** through which **groundwater** flows. Thoroughly wash and rinse the gravel. Clean off powdery deposits. Cover the surface of the large tub with 2 inches of gravel (5 centimeters).

2 Now make a slope to the gravel. On one end of the tub, make a downward slope. Angle the gravel so it's ½ inch deep at the low end (1.3 centimeters). At the opposite end, form an upslope. Angle the gravel to 3 inches deep (7½ centimeters).

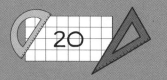

3 Combine clay and sand in the medium-sized tub, reserving some modeling clay to use later. Use a bit more clay than sand to make a grainy consistency. The gritty mixture should allow water to run freely over it. When standing, the water should gradually permeate, or pass through, the mixture. Test your mixture with water to make sure it will work.

4 Carefully add the mixture to the aquifer in the large tub. Be careful not to crush the aquifer or knock its slopes out of position.

5 Add a river. With the paint stirrer and your hands, carve a channel about ½ inch deep (1.3 centimeters) and 1 inch wide (2½ centimeters). At the slope's top, split the channel into three tributaries. These smaller rivers are separate bodies of water that join the larger one. Use the aluminum foil to line the river and tributaries. Fill them with water.

6 Build hills between the tributaries. Use modeling clay to form hills of different sizes. Place them in position.

7 Bring on the rain! Spritz the watershed with the spray bottle. What happens to the rainfall? Is the runoff clear?

8 Experiment with pollution. Sprinkle cocoa into one tributary. Spritz the watershed. What do you predict will happen? What does runoff look like now? What conclusions can you draw about pollution's impact on watersheds?

TRY THIS

Populate the watershed. Add toy houses, farms, and trees along the river. Use chunks of wood to represent buildings and businesses.

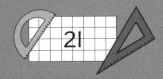

Zipping Along

SUPPLIES: *2 sturdy chairs of equal size, 9 feet of fishing line (3 meters), red permanent marker, sheet of paper, medium-sized paper cup, masking tape, scissors, paper clip, string, index card, marble, paper and pencil*

Engineers have Sir Isaac Newton to thank for their understanding of gravity. He is the English scientist, physicist, and mathematician famous for discovering gravity and the three laws of motion. Explore the engineering process as you observe Newton's First Law of Motion and the force of gravity. According to Newton's First Law of Motion, when an object is moving, it won't stop unless some force acts on it—like gravity!

1 To set up the zip line, position the chairs back to back. At the top of one chair, securely tie an end of fishing line. Angle the line downward. Tie the other end to the other chair's leg. Pull the chairs apart to create a taut line.

2 With the marker, draw a bull's-eye on the paper to make a target. Place the target flat on the floor under the lower end of the line.

3 Use masking tape to form a handle over the top of the cup to make a bucket. Uncurl the paper clip to make a hook on one end. Twist the other end of the clip tightly around the handle so it's secure. Be careful, the clip might be sharp!

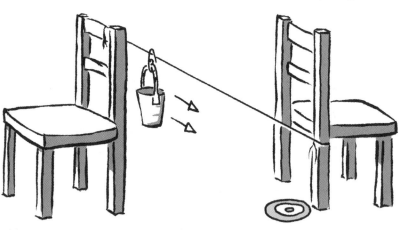

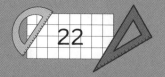

Notable Quotable

"If at first you don't succeed, try, try again."
—W. E. Hickson (1803–1870), British educational writer

4 Ready to tackle your challenge? Brainstorm ways you can use the string, masking tape, index card, and scissors to modify the cup to carry the marble down the zip line. It needs to hold the marble as it zips down the line, but that's not all. You'll need to find a way to tip the cup and release the marble so it drops onto the target.

5 With paper and pencil, design a plan. Ask questions. Will the marble ride inside the cup? On an outside ledge? A stand under it? How will the marble release?

6 Build your design and test it. Did it work the way you anticipated? How can you improve it? Evaluate the design and make modifications. Try, try again!

WORDS to KNOW

trajectory: the curve a body travels along in its path through space.

WHAT'S HAPPENING?

As the cup zips down the line, the marble gains speed as gravity pulls it. Once the marble releases, it continues at that speed. It drops to the target and slams to the ground. A force acts on it and the marble stops moving. Observe the marble drop. It moves along a curved path, even though it zipped horizontally down the line. That's its **trajectory**!

Tetrahedron Forcebuster

SUPPLIES: *paper and pencil, ruler, 6 plastic drinking straws (not the bendy type) of 3 different colors (red, blue, green, for example), scissors, string, large sewing needle*

Civil engineers rely on triangles for many constructions. It is the strongest shape. The **tetrahedron** is a shape with four triangular faces (think of the pyramids of Egypt). Test how well triangle power can resist pushing and pulling forces. Ask an adult to help you thread the sewing needle and supervise as you use it. Connect the straws tightly. They should be rigid, not loose. It is helpful if all straws meeting at one vertex have a different color. That's the point where the angles intersect.

WORDS to KNOW

tetrahedron: a pyramid containing four triangular faces.

1 With the paper, pencil, and ruler, draw a tetrahedron to visualize its shape and connections. You can use the picture on the next page as a guide. Notice each vertex.

BASE STRAWS r b g

2 Build a 3-D model. Put one straw of each color on the table, forming an equilateral triangle for the base of your tetrahedron.

3 Cut off a 60-inch length of string (152 centimeters) and thread it through the needle.

DID YOU KNOW?

Alexander Graham Bell, the inventor of the telephone, invented the tetrahedron!

4 Hold the other three straws (one of each color) above the base straws. Use the diagram and thread pattern shown here to thread the straws and build your tetrahedron. The base straws are labeled with lowercase letters and the upright straws are capital letters. Start by threading one of the upright straws (R), then thread two base straws (g and r), two upright straws (G and R), two base straws (b and r), two upright straws (B and G), two base straws (b and g), and one last upright straw (B).

5 Make sure all of the sides are threaded tightly. Securely knot the string at the vertex to connect the straws.

6 Predict whether your structure will resist pushing and pulling forces. Tug on different connections. Does it maintain its triangular shape?

THREAD PATTERN:
R-g-r-G-R-b-r-B-G-b-g-B

UPRIGHT STRAWS
(R, G, B)

BASE STRAWS
(r, g, b)

B G R r g b

TRY THIS

Build other shapes, such as a rhombus and a cube. Compare results. Test different building materials including toothpicks, marshmallows, and gumdrops. How do materials impact the results?

BUILDING BIG: THE PHYSICS OF CANALS

DO YOU THINK YOU COULD LIVE WITHOUT WATER?
It's essential for survival. But its power can be ferocious and
unpredictable. Since ancient times, people have tackled the
monumental task of moving and managing water. They
have changed its flow or dammed it up, diverting it through
rolling hills and over and around steep mountains.

Canals are man-made water channels. Some are **navigable** and act like massive water highways for **barges** moving tons of **cargo**. Others are **aqueducts** that supply safe drinking water. Irrigation canals move water to soil for farming.

When you look at a canal, you might just see a huge ditch filled with water. But canals are more complicated than they seem. Because canals present complex building and design challenges, there's a lot going on below ground in a canal.

WORDS to KNOW

navigable: deep and wide enough for a boat or ship to pass through.

barge: a boat with a flat bottom used to carry loads on canals and rivers.

cargo: things carried by ship.

aqueduct: a pipe or channel that moves water over long distances.

riverbed: the area between the banks of a river ordinarily covered by water.

bank: the sloped side of a river.

CHANNEL IT

A channel can be natural or man-made, or a combination of both. A natural channel is made up of a **riverbed** and its **banks**. But engineers can also design man-made channels that form most of a canal's length. The purpose of a man-made channel is to keep the steep, sloping banks of a body of water from caving in.

DID YOU KNOW?

One barge can haul 2,000 tons of cargo at once. That's 4 million pounds (1,814,370 kilograms)—equal to the weight of 50 trucks! Moving this amount of cargo by barge uses a lot less fuel than moving the same amount of cargo by truck.

WORDS to KNOW

geometric: using straight lines and simple shapes such as circles or squares.

trapezoid: a four-sided shape with two **parallel** sides and two non-parallel sides.

parallel: lines extending in the same direction, keeping the same distance between them.

erosion: the gradual wearing away of soil by water or ice.

Engineers design channels with **geometric** shapes. The shape they choose depends on where a channel is built and the building materials used. If a channel is built in an earth bank, a **trapezoid** is the best choice.

A trapezoidal channel is wide at the top where water flows and narrow at the riverbed.

Earth banks will shift and move. With sloped sides, a trapezoid keeps banks stable. For channels built of strong materials such as steel columns, stone, or concrete, engineers choose rectangles with their sturdy vertical sides.

Today, engineers don't have to rely on nature to keep channels from leaking. While reeds and other stalky plants protect squishy riverbanks, waterproof liners do a better job. Liners made of concrete or other materials, such as a sticky tar called bitumen, protect riverbanks from **erosion**.

DID YOU KNOW?

Construction workers have to perform heavy jobs in the middle of flowing waterways. How do they do it? Inside **cofferdams**! These are temporary watertight enclosures. They allow workers to pump an area of a river dry and expose the riverbed. From a dry construction site, workers can lay foundations and pipes.

BRIDGES AND TUNNELS

Bridges and tunnels are other important canal structures. Tunnels provide access through natural obstacles such as mountains or man-made obstacles such as buildings. Tunnel engineers dig into soft ground and blast through hard rock and beneath water.

Through hilly areas made of soft earth, workers can dig out **cuttings** with rugged bulldozers and other giant earthmovers. A dozer's front blade pushes huge loads of rubble and its rear claws tear apart mounds of rock and earth. But if hills are steep and made of harder rock, then a true tunnel is **excavated** with a tunnel **boring** machine, or TBM.

WORDS to KNOW

cofferdam: a temporary watertight structure pumped dry and used for underwater construction.

cutting: a small, man-made valley cut through a hill.

excavate: to dig out earth and soil.

boring: making a hole.

A bridge spans natural obstacles like rivers and man-made obstacles including roads and canals. Some canal bridges allow people to walk across or bicycle along. Others are large enough to provide roadways for motorists.

ALL LEGS ON DECK

Have you ever walked along a canal? You might be on the **towpath** that horses once walked to power barges up and down canals. At a tunnel, the horses were walked over the hill to the other side. Workers lay on top of the barge and used their feet to push against the side of the tunnel and walk the barge through. This was called legging.

WORDS to KNOW

towpath: a path along a river or canal used for towing barges and boats.

lock: a step that allows barges to move up or down a canal.

vessel: a ship or large boat.

inclined plane: an angled surface.

ALL LOCKED UP

Barges can't travel uphill, so canals must be level. Just as stairs connect an underground basement with a ground-level room, **locks** link two segments or bodies of water that are at different levels. They're like huge, watertight stairways. Gates at both ends open and close to raise and lower the water levels. This allows **vessels** and barges to be lifted or lowered with the shape of the land.

A canal is an inclined plane. Its locks move barges without using a great deal of energy.

DID YOU KNOW?

Ramp up! Inclined planes help people in many ways. Spot them in wheelchair ramps, ladders, staircases, and roller coasters.

WORDS to KNOW

upstream: against the direction of a stream's **current**, toward its source.

current: the steady movement of water in a certain direction.

sluice gate: a gate that opens to allow water to flow in and out of locks.

downstream: in the direction of a stream's current, away from its source.

How does a barge journey **upstream**? With gravity's help! At the lower level, a barge enters the lock. All the lock's gates close and the chamber becomes watertight. Then the upper **sluice gates** open. With gravity's force, water from the higher level enters the lock. As water inside the lock reaches the same level as the canal's upstream water level, the barge slowly rises with the level of the water. The upper gates open and the barge moves out on the new level.

A **downstream** journey is reversed. At the upper level, a barge enters the lock and the gates shut. The lower sluices open and water flows out. Inside the lock, the water level—and the barge—reach the same level on both sides of the lower gates. The lower gates open and the barge sails downstream.

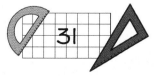

ARCHIMEDES' SCREW

Archimedes (287–212 **BCE**) was a Greek mathematician and inventor. He was a master problem solver who created inventions that helped others. Sound like an engineer? Well, he was one of the first! King Heron often called on Archimedes to tackle challenges. So when the king's magnificent luxury ship sprang a leak, he looked to Archimedes for help.

The result was the now-famous Archimedes' screw to pump mucky water out of the ship's giant hull. How did it work? The Archimedes' screw is made of a hollow tube with a continuous screw inside. A person placed one end of the tube into the water, then turned a crank that turned the screw. As the screw turned, water moved up the tube along the spinning spiral. The Archimedes' screw moved water with a lot less work than hoisting buckets of water by hand! It worked such wonders that people started using it to pump rainwater and irrigate crops.

WORDS to KNOW

BCE: put after a date, BCE stands for Before Common Era and counts down to zero. CE stands for Common Era and counts up from zero. These non-religious terms correspond to BC and AD.

The machine proved ingenious. We still rely on it, with present-day twists of course. In modern water treatment plants, similar devices lift wastewater. Today, the screw is part of the wild Shipwreck Rapids ride at Sea World in San Diego, California! It lifts water for the 4-mile seafaring amusement park adventure (8 kilometers).

CANAL PHYSICS

With so many structures involved in canals, engineers apply different principles of physical science. According to Newton's third law of motion, "For every action (force) there is an equal and opposite reaction (force)." This means that keeping canals from collapsing relies on balancing forces. If one force is stronger than the other, the structure could fail. The pulling forces of **tension** and the pushing forces of **compression** are constantly working on these structures.

WORDS to KNOW

tension: a pulling force that pulls or stretches material outward.

compression: a pushing force that squeezes or presses material inward.

buoyancy: a force that allows an object to float in liquid.

volume: the amount of space inside an object.

OH BUOYANCY!

When constructing locks, engineers use principles of **buoyancy**. This is the upward force that allows an object to float in liquid. How does a monstrous vessel or hefty barge stay afloat? With a large **volume** of water! You won't float in a bathtub because the volume of water is too low. But what happens when you take a plunge into a pool's deep end? With a much greater volume of water, you can bob on the surface.

Engineers need to make sure that there's enough water in locks to keep boats from sinking!

Archimedes' principle explains why. When you get into that bathtub of water, the water level rises, right? Your body is taking up space so the water has to go somewhere. This is **displacement**.

For an object to float, it must displace, or move, an amount of water equal to its own weight. If the same weight in water pushes back up against the object, it will float. If the amount of force pushing up against the object is not equal to the object's weight, the object sinks. It sinks because gravity's force pulls the object down and there's not enough force pushing the object back up. So a rock sinks because it doesn't displace enough water.

A boat floats because it displaces loads of water.

WORDS to KNOW

displacement: when something is moved by an object taking its place.

DISPLACED WATER

TRY THIS

When water freezes, it expands. It takes up more space than water in liquid form. That's why water pipes sometimes burst during very cold weather. Fill a clear plastic cup almost to the top with room temperature water. Place it in the freezer. Take it out the next day and notice what happened.

LEONARDO DA VINCI

Leonardo da Vinci enjoyed dazzling creativity as an artist, but he was also an architect, engineer, inventor, and scientist. A kind and gentle man with an outgoing, chatty personality, Leonardo loved nature. Water, the world's source of power at the time, intrigued him. He applied knowledge of buoyancy and invented early scuba gear. His creation proved remarkably similar to today's modern gear. It consisted of a leather diving suit and a hood to protect the diver's head. From the hood's nose section, two cane tubes connected to a cork bell. The buoyant bell bobbed on the water's surface.

Leonardo was afraid people would use his invention "for evil in war." The invention was revealed only after his death in 1519, when people studied his journals.

DID YOU KNOW?

The screw used in Archimedes' screw is a simple machine. Other simple machines are the inclined plane, **lever**, pulley, wedge, and wheel and axle. Simple machines make work easier. A screw is actually an inclined plane that winds around itself. Twisty jar lids and light bulbs that rotate into sockets are examples of screws.

WORDS to KNOW

lever: a bar that rests on a support and lifts or moves things.

Whatever Floats Your Paddle Wheel Boat

SUPPLIES: *duct tape, ½ gallon cardboard milk carton, 5 rubber bands, 2 pencils, cork, knife, scissors, 2-liter plastic soda bottle, tub of water*

**Observe Newton's third law of motion in action!
The paddles push the water backward, moving the
boat forward with equal and opposite force.**

HINT: Try this outside in a stream or under a gutter after a rainfall.

1 Tape the top of the carton shut. Wrap four rubber bands around the bottom. Lie the carton down and on opposite sides, slip a pencil through the bands. About half of the pencils' length should extend past the end of the carton.

2 Ask an adult to use the knife to make four evenly spaced slits along the length of the cork. Use scissors to cut two square paddles from the bottle with sides equal to the cork's length.

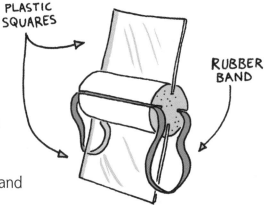

PLASTIC SQUARES

RUBBER BAND

3 Slide the paddles into opposite cork slits. Slide a rubber band into the other two slits so there is a loop at both ends of the cork with the rest of the rubber band gripped by the cork.

DID YOU KNOW?

Ancient Chinese paddle wheel boats had sides that hid 20 paddle wheels and the boatmen powering them. From land, it looked like the boats were gliding magically along!

Notable Quotable

"I have not failed. I've just found 10,000 ways that won't work."
—Thomas Edison (1847–1932), American inventor of the electric light, motion picture camera, phonograph, and many other inventions.

4 Mount the cork paddle wheel by slipping each loop over a pencil. To test your vessel, wind the paddle wheel and place the boat in the tub. Does it sink, tip, flip, or stay afloat? Notice what happens when you wind the wheel to the right. Does it move forward or backward? Wind it to the left. It should move in the opposite direction.

5 Evaluate and modify the design, then rebuild your boat with your own innovative ideas for an improved vessel.

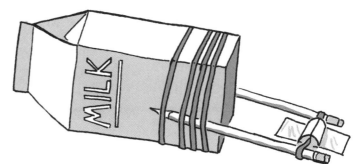

TRY THIS

Explore how Archimedes' principle and Newton's third law of motion work together to make an ice cube float. Fill a cup halfway with water and drop an ice cube into it. To make way for the ice, water gets displaced. As it does, it pushes up against gravity's downward force on the ice cube with an equal and opposite force.

Move It!

SUPPLIES: *small bag, 1 cup dried beans (8 ounces), twist tie, 6 books, scissors, rubber band, ruler*

An inclined plane is a flat surface that is sloped or tilted. Like all simple machines, it reduces the amount of force necessary to overcome gravity and move a load. Will a straight surface or an inclined plane make it easier to hoist a bag of beans?

1 Make the load. Fill the bag with beans and tightly secure the bag with the twist tie. Now, you have a problem to solve! How can you hoist the bag without touching it?

2 Stack five books. Make an inclined plane by slanting the sixth against the stack.

3 With scissors, cut apart the rubber band. Tightly tie one end to the bag's top. Will it be easier to hoist the bag by lifting it straight up or with the inclined plane? Ask questions and form a **hypothesis**.

WORDS to KNOW

hypothesis: an unproven idea that tries to explain certain facts or observations.

data: information, facts, and numbers from tests and experiments.

4 Test the straight-up method first. Predict how much effort you'll use to hoist the bag. Hold one end of the rubber band and raise the bag straight up to place it on top of the stack, being careful not to snap the band. Measure the extended band's length. How far (in inches or centimeters) did the rubber band need to stretch for the load to reach the top of the book stack? How much force did you use?

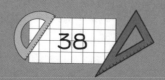

5 To test the inclined plane, place the bag at the bottom. Hold one end of the rubber band. Slowly pull the bag up the plane so the band doesn't snap. When the bag reaches the plane's upper edge, nearly at the top, measure the extended band. How much force did you use?

6 Complete the chart with your numbers. This is your **data**. Describe what took place during each test and compare the results with the rubber band lengths. Analyze your data. Draw conclusions about how far the rubber band stretches and the amount of forced used.

Straight-up Measurement	Force Rating (1–10)	Inclined-plane Measurement	Force Rating (1–10)

TRY THIS

Play Push-Me-Pull-You! Act out compression and tension with a buddy. Stand back to back. Lightly bend one knee and keep your other leg straight but not locked. Gently lean against each other's upper back and push. How does compression feel? This time, face each other. Extend your arms and grasp each other's hands. Carefully rock back on your heels, pulling back until you are both balanced. This is tension. How does tension contrast with compression?

Barge In!

SUPPLIES: *scissors, foam egg carton, glue, craft sticks, cardboard egg carton, tub of water*

Oh, bouy! For an object to float, it must be denser than what it's floating in. Build an eggs-traordinary barge.

1 To build the bottom, carefully cut the lid from the egg carton. From the remaining portion, cut away a section of four connected cups. Flip the lid upside down.

WORDS to KNOW

dense: how tightly the matter in an object is packed.

2 Glue craft sticks across the upside-down lid to build a deck. Completely cover the surface. Glue one or two sticks off either end of the deck to extend it.

3 Glue the 4-cup section to the deck with the open end of the cups down. While the foam barge is drying, build another barge the same way with a cardboard egg carton. Let it dry completely.

4 Predict whether your barges will sink or float. To take the buoyancy test, place the foam carton barge in the tub of water. What happens? How does foam material impact buoyancy?

5 Compare the building materials of your two barges. What happens when you place the cardboard carton barge in the tub of water? Which carton gets waterlogged? Which is more buoyant? Why?

Rockin' Raisins

SUPPLIES: *2 clear identical drinking glasses, tap water, 12 plump raisins, clear carbonated beverage such as seltzer water or lemon-lime soda*

Will raisins boogie when you drop them into water and a carbonated drink?

1 Fill one glass with tap water. Do bubbles rise from the bottom? Plop in six raisins. Predict what will happen when you let the glass stand for 5 minutes. Do the raisins sink or float?

2 Slowly pour the carbonated beverage into the second glass. Do bubbles rise? You probably notice fizzing as carbon dioxide gas releases. Drop in six raisins. Do they sink or float? Wait 5 minutes. How do the raisins respond? Let the beverage sit until it no longer bubbles. What happens now?

3 Compare the raisins in each glass. Do they respond to the liquids differently? How do bubbles from the release of carbon dioxide gas make raisins buoyant?

WHAT'S HAPPENING?

In both glasses, the raisins are denser than liquid and sink to the bottom. In the fizzy glass, bubbles grab onto the raisins' surface. Buoyancy increases and the raisins drift to the surface on a trail of bubbles. When the bubbles hit the surface, they pop, and gas escapes into the air. Buoyancy fizzles away. Raisins, no matter how plump, sink to the bottom as they become too waterlogged to float. Sogginess weights them down. Test other items! Will mini marshmallows rock out? Dried pasta? Blueberries?

Explore Buoyancy With a Cartesian Diver

SUPPLIES: *64-ounce plastic bottle with cap (1890 milliliters), tap water, plastic tub, hex nut, plastic pipette (chemical dropper), scissors, glass of tap water, tweezers, measuring spoon, table salt*

When you dive into a pool, you hold your breath and rise to the surface. Buoyant force moves you up. A human body's average density is close to the density of water. The weight of displaced water balances your body weight. Demonstrate gravity and buoyancy with a Cartesian diver. HINT: This is splashy! The tub should be deep enough to catch plenty of water.

1 Make a body of water. Fill the bottle with tap water. Set aside the cap and place the bottle upright into the tub.

2 Prepare the diver. Place the hex nut over the pipette's open end to provide necessary weight. Move the nut up the pipette's stem and screw it tightly against the bulb end. Carefully snip off the stem under the nut.

3 Place the pipette into the glass of water. Fill the pipette halfway with water. Your diver is ready to take the plunge! Place the diver, hex nut down, into the bottle. Firmly screw the bottle lid in place.

HEX NUT

4 Place your hands around the bottle and squeeze firmly. Does the diver sink? When you squeeze the bottle, you decrease air volume inside the pipette. You increase pressure in the water system.

DID YOU KNOW?

An object's density determines buoyancy. In the bottle, buoyant force and gravity battle it out to control where the diver moves.

Notable Quotable

"Water is the driving force of all nature."
—*Leonardo da Vinci (1452–1519) famed Italian artist who painted the Mona Lisa*

5 Release the bottle. That releases pressure in the water system. Does the diver float to the top? Air volume in the pipette increases and displaces some water. The pipette's density increases. It becomes buoyant. If your diver stayed at the bottom, lightly tap the bottom of the bottle to give the diver a boost.

6 If the diver doesn't sink at first, try, try again! Use tweezers to retrieve the pipette. What problem do you need to solve? Try adjusting the amount of water inside. What happens?

7 Try to get the diver to hover in the middle of the bottle. Experiment with different levels of pressure on the bottle's sides. What works best?

8 Slowly untwist the bottle cap and remove it. Add 4 teaspoons of salt (20 milliliters), which increases water's density. Screw the cap back on. Squeeze the bottle's side. Try to move the diver to the bottom. With greater density, is it easier or harder to do?

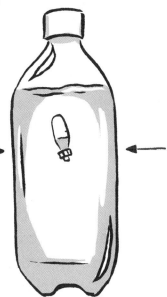

TRY THIS

Build the diver again. This time, modify the water temperature. Use hotter or colder water. Predict how temperature will impact results. You can also try making a super-simple diver! Use a full plastic condiment package. Mayo or mustard?

AMAZING CANALS

FROM EARLY BASINS THAT CAPTURED AND HELD FLOODWATERS
to the ancient waterworks in America's Southwest,
canals have changed the course of waterways and even
connected oceans. Some of these amazing feats of
engineering have even changed the course of history.

ANCIENT EGYPT AND NILE FLOODWATERS

Egypt receives almost no rainfall. Its civilization has always depended on Egypt's only real source of water, the Nile River. Lining the banks of the world's longest river is nearly 4,200 miles of **fertile** soil (6,760 kilometers). In a parched brown landscape, it paints a lush green valley. Nearly all of ancient Egypt's astonishing cultural achievements rose along the Nile's riverbanks.

WORDS to KNOW

fertile: good for growing crops.

equator: the imaginary line around the earth, halfway between the North and South Poles.

silt: fine soil rich in **nutrients**.

nutrients: the substances in food and soil that keep animals and plants healthy and growing.

The Nile originates far from Egypt in the tropical highlands of Burundi, south of the **equator**. Swollen by storms in Ethiopia, it flows north through the Sahara Desert before draining into the Mediterranean Sea. The Nile is one of Earth's most predictable rivers. It floods continually for about 100 days each year. Every June, melting snow thousands of miles from Egypt triggers the flooding, drenching the cracked, dry Nile Valley and depositing fertile black **silt**.

More than 4,000 years ago, engineers devised systems to capture the river's waters at their peak. They built canals to irrigate fields far from the riverbanks. To get water to the canals, they built basins that filled with water during the flood. These basins were like giant containers with flat bottoms that trapped as much water as possible.

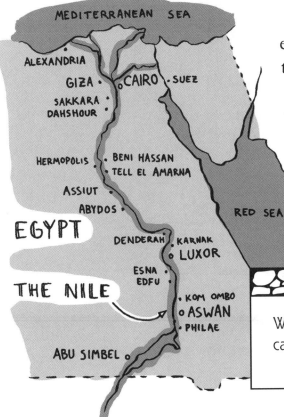

DID YOU KNOW?

When ancient civilizations in the Middle East built canals for irrigation and to deliver drinking water, laborers dug these structures by hand.

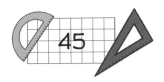

WORDS to KNOW

floodgate: a gate in a waterway that is used to control the flow of water.

saturate: to soak with water.

famine: a severe shortage of food resulting in widespread hunger.

By using simple **floodgates**, engineers figured out how to refill the irrigation canals with water from the basins. Using the gates to control the water, farmers held water in their fields for about two months to **saturate** parched soil. Then they drained the water back to the Nile.

Egyptians were completely dependent on the Nile waters.

Too little water meant failed crops and **famine**. Too much meant disaster and destruction. Engineers started carving notches into vertical columns to measure the height the water reached during the floods. With this simple measuring system, called a nilometer, farmers could plan their water use for the coming year.

Notable Quotable

"Imagination is more important than knowledge."
—*Albert Einstein*

ANCIENT WATER MOVER

Ancient Egyptians invented the *shaduf* to lift water from a lower place, like a canal, to a higher place, like a field. How does a *shaduf* work? It's a lever built with a long, sturdy branch or pole balanced on a crossbeam. At the longer end is a bucket or animal skin bag to collect water. At the shorter end is a heavy **counterweight** like a rock or chunk of clay. The counterweight balances the weight of the water in the bucket, which makes raising the water nearly effortless.

To operate the *shaduf*, the worker tugs a rope attached to the long end. The machine swings into action with a sweeping, seesaw motion. The bucket fills and the counterweight easily hoists it up. The worker swings the pole around and empties the bucket into the irrigation ditch.

WORDS to KNOW

counterweight: an equal weight that balances an object.

DID YOU KNOW?

The *shaduf* is still used in Egypt, Romania, and India, where it's called a *denkli* or *paecottah*.

EARLIEST AMERICAN CANALS: LAS CAPAS—THE LAYERS

- **TYPE:** network of canals
- **PURPOSE:** supplied water to fields for crops
- **CONSTRUCTION DATE:** 1200 BCE

For years, confused archaeologists couldn't figure out how ancient farmers grew **maize** in one of the hottest, driest deserts in America. After years of digging for evidence of irrigation in the Southwest's Sonoran Desert, they finally unearthed the answer in 2009. With specially designed backhoes, they excavated Las Capas waterworks. The crisscrossing structure runs along the outskirts of present-day Tucson, Arizona.

WORDS to KNOW

maize: corn.

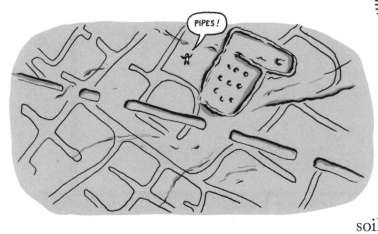

The Las Capas network of canals is the earliest irrigation system in the United States. With stone hand tools and wooden digging sticks, ancient people chiseled the desert soil, called caliche. This mixture of rock and clay and sand is hard as concrete! Ancient engineers routed water from the Santa Cruz River through eight different canals across 100 acres of fields (325 hectares). Farmers grew cotton, squash, maize, and a high-protein grain called amaranth.

You can still see ancient planting holes!

This incredible discovery rewrites United States history. Early inhabitants were once thought to be hunter-gatherers. But as archaeologist Suzanne Fish says, "There's so much intensive labor there it's hard to see builders going off and leaving it." By diverting water, ancient engineers advanced civilization.

Archaeologist James Vint agrees. "This puts them on the ground and anchors them to a place . . . It requires a high level of social organization to operate a large irrigated system." The excavation team also dug up pit houses. Workers who tended fields and canals probably lived there.

ERIE CANAL: NEW YORK, UNITED STATES

- **TYPE:** towpath with lift locks
- **LENGTH:** 363 miles between Buffalo and Albany
- **PURPOSE:** transport cargo such as grain, lumber, produce
- **CONSTRUCTION DATES:** 1817–1825
- **DATES OF OPERATION:** 1825–1918

In 1808, New York City mayor Dewitt Clinton (1769–1828) proposed an innovative idea—to construct a massive canal linking Lake Erie and other Great Lakes with the Atlantic Seaboard. He believed the waterway would improve transportation through the country's Midwest. With a canal, America could expand and grow. The canal would not only link bodies of water. It would link manufacturing in the East with raw materials in the West.

Hauling goods by rickety horse-drawn wagons across treacherous, rutted trails was dangerous, expensive, and slow.

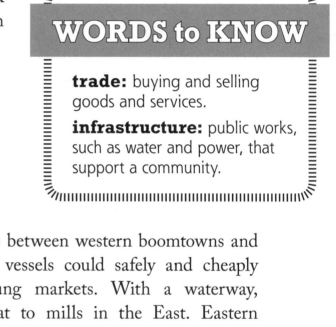

WORDS to KNOW

trade: buying and selling goods and services.

infrastructure: public works, such as water and power, that support a community.

A waterway would open **trade** between western boomtowns and eastern cities. Barges and other vessels could safely and cheaply transport goods between far-flung markets. With a waterway, western settlers could ship wheat to mills in the East. Eastern factories could sell manufactured goods, including hoes and shovels, to those in search of gold in the West. At nearly 400 miles long (644 kilometers), the canal would extend across the entire state of New York, connecting Lake Erie and the Hudson River. The Erie Canal would be the country's first superhighway, the first major **infrastructure** project.

Notable Quotable

"Long before railroads, interstate highways, or jets, the Erie Canal opened the interior of North America and shaped the future of a young nation."
—*Erie Canalway National Heritage Corridor website*

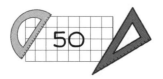

OBSTACLES AND PROBLEMS

People scoffed at Clinton's idea. President Thomas Jefferson declared it "little short of madness." Skeptics called it "Clinton's Big Ditch." They pointed out obstacles, like the craggy Appalachian Mountains, blocking the way. Immense trees in huge forests would need to be chopped down and the massive stumps would need to be unearthed. Tons of earth would need to be hauled away. And how would they build the canal through hills and across valleys? These were all huge challenges for a young nation lacking experienced engineers!

Clinton was determined not to let difficulties stand in his way. When people called his project Clinton's Folly, he persisted. By 1811,

DID YOU KNOW?

Within nine years, canal tolls paid for the cost of building the Erie Canal.

Clinton became the Erie Canal commissioner and by 1817, he was New York's governor. He vigorously rallied others to support his plan, convincing the government to authorize $7 million to construct the canal. With great pride, Clinton officiated at the groundbreaking ceremony.

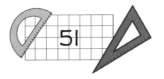

Clinton may have been the mover and shaker behind the Erie Canal, but who actually moved the earth without the massive earthmovers we depend on today? Working for about a dollar a day, thousands of Irish, British, and German **immigrants** joined American workers. All endured backbreaking labor. Horses pulled plows to excavate soil. Workers attacked the ground with axes and picks. Toiling in the hot summer sun, they scraped away rocky dirt. During icy winters, they hoisted shovel loads of frozen earth into carts. Laborers hitched oxen and horses to the carts to haul the dirt to other areas, where workers dumped it.

WORDS to KNOW

immigrant: a person who comes to settle in a new country.

FIFTEEN YEARS ON THE ERIE CANAL

The Erie Canal was used for more than trade. Passengers traveled on the Erie Canal purely for the pleasure of enjoying a leisurely cruise. Boys called "hoggees" tended the mules that hauled the barges along the towpaths of the canal. Have you ever heard the song "Fifteen Years on the Erie Canal?" In 1905, songwriter Thomas S. Allen composed the popular folk song after engine power had taken over for mule power. He recalled the good old days of mule barges. The chorus, "Low bridge, everybody down" had a special message. Barge passengers ducked under low-slung, skull-cracking bridges for safe passage!

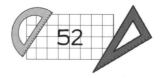

The project was like a school of engineering. Everyone learned on the job and from their mistakes. With hand drills and explosive powder, workers blasted through rock and cut through cliffs. They constructed 18 aqueducts and 83 locks. They developed hydraulic cement to harden underwater.

For nine long years the project limped on. People worried that the work would never end and that Clinton's Big Ditch would just remain an ugly hole in the ground. But mile by mile, engineers and laborers completed the Erie Canal in 1825. During a 10-day celebration, Clinton cruised its entire length in a vessel named the *Seneca Chief*. A **flotilla** sailed with him. One vessel in the fleet, *Noah's Ark*, sailed with a bear, two eagles, and two fawns aboard! At each town on the journey, people cheered and shot off cannons while marching bands blared rousing tunes.

WORDS to KNOW

flotilla: a number of vessels.

DID YOU KNOW?

Before setting sail from Buffalo, New York, for his celebratory cruise, Clinton scooped a barrelful of Lake Erie's water. Arriving in New York City, he poured it into the Atlantic Ocean. The symbolic tribute honored the amazing connection of two distant ports and a marvel of engineering!

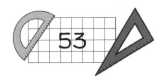

Clinton's bright idea became a reality and it benefited a new nation. Afterwards, a brief canal craze swept North America and people dug canals across the eastern United States and Canada. During the 1850s, canal mania fizzled when railroads—a faster method of transportation—connected distant parts of the continent.

DID YOU KNOW?

Many New Yorkers built the Erie Canal. And the canal built New York! After construction, New York shone as the United States' most prosperous seaport. It grew into the most populous city in the country and in time became the center of world trade.

AMAZING CANALS ACROSS THE GLOBE

GRAND CANAL (Present-day Beijing and Hang Zhou, China, 486 BCE–610 CE, with further construction through the 1960s)

- Connects the Yangtze River Valley with the Yellow River Valley. The canal is 1,085 miles long (1,747 kilometers) and 2 to 15 feet deep (½–4½ meters).

- Originally built to ship grain to people and armies.

- Slaves endured grueling conditions and crude building techniques to construct the original structure. About 3 million people died during construction.

With 60 bridges and 24 locks, China's Grand Canal is the world's longest man-made waterway and its oldest working canal.

KARA KUM CANAL (Turkmenistan, 1954–1988)

- Feeds land from the Amu Darya River to Ashgabat, 870 miles away (1,400 kilometers).

- Provides irrigation for a landlocked nation that is 80 percent desert.

- The world's longest irrigation canal delivers water for cattle raising and nut, fig, and olive crops. **Toxic** pesticides make the water dangerous for drinking.

WORDS to KNOW

toxic: something that is poisonous.

isthmus: a narrow strip of land bordered by water on both sides, joining two larger land areas.

PANAMA CANAL (Panama, 1882–1914)

- Links the Atlantic and Pacific Oceans by crossing the **Isthmus** of Panama in Central America. The canal is 50.7 miles long (82 kilometers) and 41 feet deep (12 meters).

- The international waterway enables ships to avoid the dangerous voyage around South America's Cape Horn, saving 8,000 miles (12,874 kilometers).

- From 1821, Panama was part of Columbia, which rejected a United States proposal for canal rights. In 1903, under President Teddy Roosevelt, the United States backed Panama in a revolution. Panama's new government allowed the United States to construct the canal and control the Canal Zone.

SUEZ CANAL (Egypt, 1859–1869)

- Links the Red Sea and the Mediterranean Sea. The canal is 104 miles long (168 kilometers) and 64 feet deep (19.5 meters).

- The waterway enables ships to avoid the long voyage around the Cape of Good Hope in South Africa, saving 6,000 miles (9,656 kilometers).

- This engineering marvel parted the desert with a ribbon of water, a dream people held since ancient times!

Each year 25,000 ships, including huge oil tankers, travel the Suez Canal.

GRAND CANAL (Venice, Italy, date of construction unknown)

- Divides the city of Venice into two areas. The canal is 2 miles long (3 kilometers) and 17 feet deep (5 meters).

- The Grand Canal is a major travel waterway in the city, like the Main Street of most towns. Water taxis and the famous boats called gondolas take people from one place to another and on tours of the canals.

- Venice is a chain of 118 islands, linked by a web of canals. The Grand Canal is a natural channel that forms an s-shaped waterway in a beautiful, historic city. Funeral barges in Venice transport the dead to an island cemetery.

All Locked Up

SUPPLIES: *scissors, sturdy foam sheets or waterproof cardboard, rectangular plastic container such as a dish tub, small toy boat, pitcher of water, measuring cup*

Emptying a full lock or filling an empty one is known as "turning." The rectangular chamber of a lock has watertight gates at both ends. When a vessel enters one section, the gate closes behind it. The opposite gate is opened and, with gravity's force, water either enters or leaves the lock to meet the water level in the next section. The opposite gate opens and the vessel sails to the new waterway. Build your own model lock and experiment with "turning" it.

1 Construct sluice gates. Cut two pieces of foam sheet or waterproof cardboard to fit the width of the plastic container. Make sure the pieces fit tightly across the bottom and sides inside the container.

2 Insert the sluice gates into the container to form three sections. Arrange the sluice gate pieces to stand perpendicular to the container's bottom.

3 Fill the lock. Pour equal amounts of water into the container's first and second sections. Make sure the water levels are equal. When you pour water into the third section, pour an amount higher or lower than in the other sections.

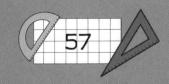

4 Place the toy boat in the first section. "Open" a sluice gate by removing the gate between the first and second sections. Position the vessel in the second section. Replace the sluice gate behind it.

5 With the pitcher and measuring cup, add or remove water in the second section until it's equal to the third section's level. When the sections are at equal levels, remove the sluice gate between them. "Sail" your vessel through the lock!

Waterproof or Waterlogged?

SUPPLIES: *cookie sheet or cake pan, eyedropper, glass of water, pencil, paper, scissors, test materials such as aluminum foil, bubble wrap, cardboard, rags, newspaper, paper towels, plastic wrap, wax paper*

Canal liners must be waterproof. Test different materials to predict which are waterproof and which get waterlogged.

1 Set up a test site. Place the cookie sheet on a sturdy surface. Fill the eyedropper all the way with water from the glass.

2 Make a chart like the one here. Note each test material and predict whether each will be waterproof or waterlogged when you drip water onto it.

3 Start testing! Place a sheet of foil across the cake pan and drip water from the dropper onto it. What happens?

4 Test other materials. Cut, tear, or drape them to fit over the cookie sheet or cake pan. Analyze the data. What conclusions do you draw about waterproof and waterlogged materials? How many drops does it take for different materials to get waterlogged?

DID YOU KNOW?

Venice doesn't have a sewer system. Household wastes flow into canals where twice-daily tides flush wastes out to sea.

Materials Assessment Chart

Material	Prediction	# of Drops	Waterproof or Waterlogged

TRY THIS

Use trial and error to modify the materials. Transform them from waterlogged to waterproof. Can you think of other materials to test?

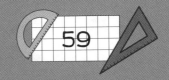

Spinning Bucket Trick

SUPPLIES: *plastic water bucket with a strong handle, water*

Canals are more than marvels of engineering. Many are so much a part of a location that we can't imagine some places without them. Artists, composers, and writers gain inspiration from the magnificent canals in Venice, the "City of Water." In 1500, Leonardo da Vinci lived and worked in Venice. The gorgeous "water city" is comprised of over 100 small islands stitched together with over 150 canals. High tides from the Adriatic Sea deluge Venice every year between November and March. During the *acqua alta*, or high water season, even the streets turn into canals!

Several factors contribute to high waters. Both the pulling of gravity and the spinning of centrifugal force are involved. Experiment with centrifugal force in this famous science trick! **HINT:** Until you perfect your swinging skills, you'll probably get wet!

1 Predict what will happen when you fill the bucket with water and swing it over your head. Test your prediction.

2 Test the bucket's handle. Make sure it's sturdy and secure. Fill the bucket halfway with water. Stand in a wide open outdoor area where you are away from people and pets. Make sure there's nothing in your way before you start swinging.

3 Grasp the bucket by the handle. Extend your arm all the way down your side. Don't lock your elbow. Allow some "give."

DID YOU KNOW?

The highest *acqua alta* on record happened on November 4, 1966, when the waters in Venice reached over 6 feet above sea level!

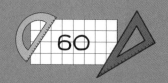

4 Swing the bucket upward in front of you. In a vertical circular motion, allow it to swing back toward the ground. Continue the rotation as you perfect your method. The trick is to spin fast enough so water remains in the bucket but not so fast that you fling the bucket out of your hand or splash water on yourself!

5 How does the trick work? Centrifugal force acts on the water during your circular motion. It holds water inside the bucket.

6 To stop, gradually slow down your motion. Bring the bucket to rest at your side. Bellisima!

CANALS ACROSS BORDERS

The 489-mile Panama Canal (77 kilometers) allows ships to cross between the Atlantic and Pacific Oceans without going all the way around the tip of South America. The United States built the Panama Canal and kept control of about 50 miles of land running right through the nation of Panama. This Canal Zone divided Panama into two parts and caused a lot of tension between the two countries. In 1999, the United States officially returned control of the Canal Zone to Panama.

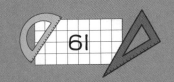

Hover, Craft!

SUPPLIES: *4-by-4-inch square of cardboard (10-by-10 centimeters), glue, empty spool, pencil, balloon, tape measure*

In 1968, hovercraft air cushion vehicles began carrying 400 passengers and 50 cars at a time across the English Channel. A hovercraft is an **amphibious** vehicle. Like amphibians in the animal world, it spends time on land and in water. A hovercraft requires little engine power because a small amount of force moves the vehicle. A hovercraft skims the water surface on a cushion of air pressure forced from a fan. The cushion of air reduces **friction**. Take flight with a nearly friction-free hovercraft!

WORDS to KNOW

amphibious: living or working both on land and in water.

friction: the force that resists motion between two objects in contact.

| Place the cardboard on a flat, sturdy surface. Glue the empty spool over the center. Allow it to dry. Push the pencil into the spool's opening and all the way through the cardboard to poke a hole in the cardboard. Put the pencil aside.

2 Stretch the balloon a few times to loosen it. Blow it up and grip its neck tightly so air doesn't leak out, but don't knot it.

PROPELLER
AIR
FAN
AIR
FAN

In the summer of 2012, deadly Typhoon Saola nearly submerged the island nation of Taipei, Taiwan. Rescuers in amphibious vehicles evacuated people stranded in homes.

3 Predict what will happen when you slip the balloon's neck over the spool's top. Does the hovercraft lift? Air pressure inside the balloon is greater than the air pressure outside. When you stretch the balloon over the spool, air swooshes down and smacks the table. Air pushes up against the cardboard, lifting it.

4 Measure the height your craft hovers from the surface. How high did it fly?

5 What if your hovercraft didn't take flight? Tweak the design. Experiment with a larger balloon. Predict what will happen. Conduct a few trials. Test how high and far your new design flies.

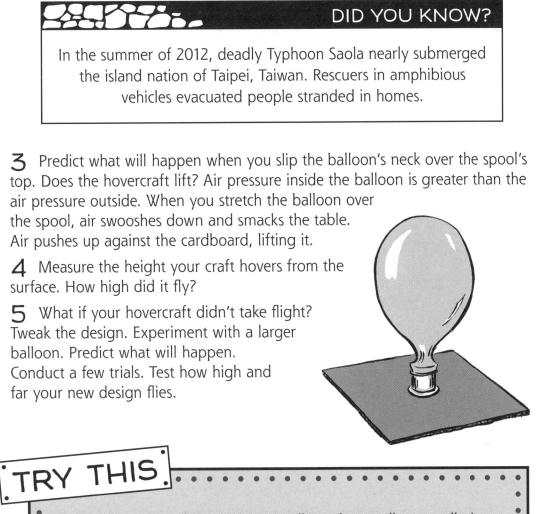

TRY THIS

Explore water's surface tension! You'll need a needle, a small piece of scratch paper, and a glass of water. Gently rest the needle in the center of the paper. Carefully place the paper into the water. In time, it becomes waterlogged and sinks to the bottom. But the needle floats! Why? Water molecules stick together to form a surface like a thin skin between the water and the air. The needle stays afloat in that surface-tension sweet spot.

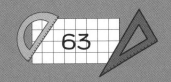

CANAL CATASTROPHES

CANALS ARE MIGHTY WATER TAMERS, BUT MOTHER NATURE is mighty too! Do you think these man-made structures can always hold up to powerful forces of nature? Hurricanes, tsunamis, and tornadoes rock canals. Even erosion and rodents gnaw at their banks. When structural failures happen, canals can crumble like sand castles. These ill-fated disasters damage the environment, cause death and injury to people and animals, and destroy entire communities.

DEADLY DISEASE: MALARIA AND THE PANAMA CANAL

Believe it or not, **malaria** nearly prevented the building of the Panama Canal. Mosquitoes that lay eggs in standing water along rivers and streams threatened everyone who labored on the canal.

WORDS to KNOW

malaria: an infectious disease transmitted by mosquito bites.

maritime: related to the sea, sailing, or shipping.

Infected mosquitoes spread malaria through their bite. Also called yellow fever, malaria strikes infected people with high fevers and vomiting and rattles its victims with teeth-chattering chills.

The Isthmus of Panama is a tropical jungle bustling with wildlife, and is a paradise for mosquitoes. Consistent high temperatures and a nine-month rainy season allow the insects to flourish in ideal breeding grounds: water.

THE WORLD'S CROSSROAD

As a key waterway for international **maritime** trade, the Panama Canal links two of the earth's great oceans, the Atlantic and the Pacific. It also connects the two giant landmasses of North and South America. For hundreds of years, people viewed the isthmus as the world's crossroad. It connected the Old World with the New World. Beginning with early European explorers, people of different nations dreamed of building a link across Central America. A link would promote trade among nations.

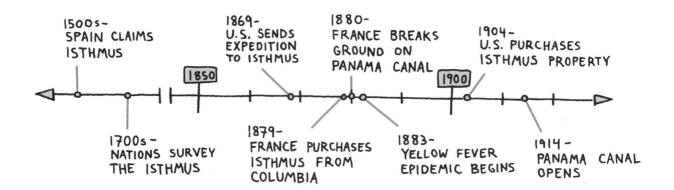

1500s–
SPAIN CLAIMS
ISTHMUS

1869–
U.S. SENDS
EXPEDITION
TO ISTHMUS

1850

1880–
FRANCE BREAKS
GROUND ON
PANAMA CANAL

1900

1904–
U.S. PURCHASES
ISTHMUS PROPERTY

1700s–
NATIONS SURVEY
THE ISTHMUS

1879–
FRANCE PURCHASES
ISTHMUS FROM
COLUMBIA

1883–
YELLOW FEVER
EPIDEMIC BEGINS

1914–
PANAMA CANAL
OPENS

The Panama Canal was centuries in the making. In the 1500s, Spanish explorers claimed the Isthmus. Two hundred years later the British **surveyed** the San Juan River between Costa Rica and Nicaragua, mapping its route to the Pacific. In 1869, United States President Ulysses S. Grant sent an expedition to the isthmus to scout water routes. After a French team surveyed the area in 1880, France purchased rights to the land from Columbia and officially broke ground.

Laborers began excavating massive amounts of earth to construct a sea-level canal. Mountainous terrain presented huge engineering hurdles. While sweltering heat and pummeling rains made the working conditions brutal, mosquitoes spread disease and death.

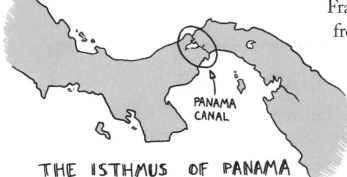

WORDS to KNOW

survey: to use math to measure angles, distances, and elevations on Earth's surfaces.

THE ISTHMUS OF PANAMA

PANAMA CANAL

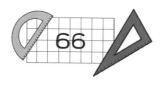

Workers excavated tons more earth than was needed for construction. The methods of the engineers were disastrously faulty. Removing the tops of hills and mounding piles of rubble on either side caused violent landslides that destroyed the construction site. In 1883, a malaria **epidemic** chopped down canal workers like trees. The workforce feared for their lives and many French engineers begged to return home. When the money ran out, the French phase of the project shriveled away.

WORDS to KNOW

epidemic: an outbreak of a disease that spreads quickly.

dynamite: a highly explosive material.

DID YOU KNOW?

Dynamite blasts, railroad collisions, drowning, disease.
How many people gave their lives to complete the Panama Canal?
Nearly 20,000 workers may have perished during the French phase.
Another 5,609 died during the American phase.

In 1904, the United States purchased rights to the land and took control of the project. Colonel William Crawford Gorgas of the U.S. Army Medical Corps engineered a plan to wipe out malaria. Focusing on destroying breeding grounds, Colonel Gorgas organized the drainage of pooled water from houses and villages. Crude oil delivered by tankers from California was poured into marshy swamps to kill mosquito eggs. The oil stunk up the work site so much that workers complained about the stench! What effect do you think the oil had on the environment?

Colonel Gorgas put mesh screens on the windows of buildings and homes to keep the mosquitoes out. His plan of action worked. It reduced malaria death rates among workers and throughout the area's population. With a successful health plan engineered, the massive construction project rolled forward.

In 1914, the United States finally completed its incredible feat of engineering. The government planned festivities to mark August 15, 1914, the Panama Canal's official opening. A fleet of international warships would sail in triumph through the canal. Sadly, the celebration never took place. The start of World War I in June 1914 prevented it.

DID YOU KNOW?

The Panama Canal has 12 locks in pairs. Each is filled with 52 million gallons of water (197 million liters). It takes a ship three hours to pass through the locks.

SHATTERED LEVEES, SHATTERED LIVES: HURRICANE KATRINA, 2005

One of the United States' most destructive disasters occurred on August 29, 2005. That sweltering day, Hurricane Katrina slammed into Louisiana's coast with 125-mile-per-hour winds (201 kilometers per hour). The tropical storm shoved enormous amounts of water from the Gulf of Mexico toward New Orleans, a city that sits mostly below sea level.

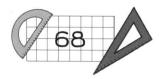

Natural forces and engineering flaws contributed to destruction from floodwaters that submerged 80 percent of the city. In New Orleans, storm water is pumped from the city through canals, to drain into Lake Pontchartrain. Levee walls above street level contain the water in the canals. During Hurricane Katrina, the drainage canals were flooded by storm surge.

WORDS to KNOW

overtop: to rise above the top of a barrier.

Stormy waters **overtopped** levees and eroded embankments. The levees crumbled, submerging neighborhoods in water. Murky floodwaters, clogged with debris, created instant lakes. In one neighborhood, the 17th Street Canal splintered into three pieces. With over 25 feet of water invading streets (8 meters), terrified people scrambled onto rooftops to escape.

In the aftermath, people in New Orleans struggled to recover. Investigators worked hard to understand what caused such mass destruction. Dr. Bob Bea, an engineer and engineering professor at the University of California, Berkeley, gathered evidence. He studied photos and scrutinized original design plans.

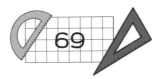

CANALS AND DAMS

What did an examination of the plans reveal?

When the canal's original engineers from the U.S. Army Corps of Engineers conducted soil tests, they discovered a weak layer of soggy soil 15 to 20 feet below sea level (4½ to 6 meters). With the hurricane's strong waves pounding this soil, it turned into what Dr. Bea called "thick pancake batter." The soil gave way, and with it the canal.

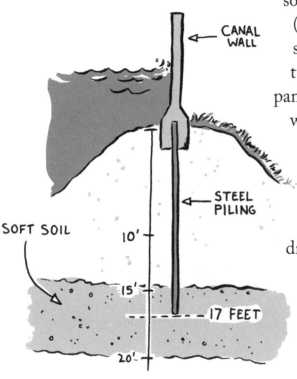

Dr. Bea believed a levee design flaw caused the collapse of the canals. The massive steel pilings anchoring the structure were driven only 17 feet deep (5 meters). If the pilings had been driven deeper, below the soggy soil layer that reached down 20 feet (6 meters), he theorized that the collapse might not have happened. The U.S. District Court ruled that the Army Corps of Engineers' flawed designs and engineering did contribute to the catastrophe. After the disaster, new, stronger levees were constructed to protect New Orleans.

DID YOU KNOW?

Hurricane Katrina remains the most expensive natural disaster in United States history. Katrina displaced more than 250,000 people, and the death toll exceeded 1,800. Total damages and repair costs are estimated to be around $125 billion dollars.

"EERILY SIMILAR": HURRICANE ISAAC, 2012

Hurricane Isaac struck on August 29, 2012, the seventh anniversary of Hurricane Katrina, unleashing a violent storm surge that made landfall over New Orleans. More than 29 inches of rain (¾ meter) pelted the city. Fast-rising floodwaters overtopped an 18-mile stretch of levees 8 to 9 feet high (about 2½ meters) in low-lying coastal Planquemines Parish, west of the Mississippi River. Tornadoes spiraled in Isaac's wake.

Rescuers battled swirling waters and downed power lines. Coast Guard choppers plucked people and pets clinging desperately to rooftops and moved them to Red Cross shelters. With half of Louisiana without power, the nation held its breath and waited for news.

Fortunately, New Orleans' strengthened levees survived the onslaught.

One 26-foot-high barrier (8 meters) built after Katrina saved the Lower 9th Ward of the city from a 15-foot storm surge (4½ meters). That was the hardest-hit area of the city during Katrina and it would have flooded again without this new $1 billion structure.

DID YOU KNOW?

The remains of what might be a Civil War ship washed ashore after Hurricane Isaac pummeled Alabama's coast.

OLD BONES AND HUNGRY CRITTERS: FAILURE OF THE TRUCKEE CANAL, 2008

On the frigid morning of January 5, 2008, 8 feet of freezing water flooded the community of Fernley, Nevada (2½ meters). The torrent destroyed 590 homes, buckled pavement, and downed power lines. Rescuers had to paddle through the streets to save people stranded in their homes. The United States government declared Fernley a state and national disaster area.

What caused the catastrophic flood? The crumbling Truckee Canal finally failed. The irrigation canal was over 100 years old and had urgently needed repair. Engineers, **geologists**, and **hydrologists** examined the evidence. Did erosion cause collapse? **Seismic** activity? Sabotage? Close study revealed the real culprits. Critters!

WORDS to KNOW

geologist: a scientist who studies the earth.

hydrologist: a scientist who studies the earth's water.

seismic: relating to earthquakes.

TRY THIS

Aging water infrastructure is a widespread problem. Maintaining safe structures is enormously expensive. Limited government funding at state and federal levels adds to challenges. Research the condition of your area's water infrastructure.

Beavers, gophers, muskrats, and other rodents had excavated the earthen canal's embankments. They had tunneled 25 feet into the ground (over 7½ meters), weakening the structure. Water **ruptured** a 50-foot breach (15 meters).

After inspecting the damage by helicopter, Nevada Senator Harry Reid called the country's attention to the aging infrastructure. "I was disturbed by what I saw," Senator Reid said. "The incredible damage caused by the canal's failure. This wasn't just an unfortunate disaster. It was an expected disaster. This was the ninth time Truckee Canal has failed. It was also the second time it failed, most likely because of rodent burrows in the canal's embankment." Repairs to the Truckee Canal are expected to take over a decade and cost more than $90 million.

DID YOU KNOW?

In 2004, over 10 million gallons of water (38 million liters) gushed over a breach in the Llangollen Canal along the Wales-England border. The canal's collapse resulted from the work of razor-clawed badgers!

THE TRAGEDY OF LOVE CANAL

William T. Love dreamed of building a model community near Niagara Falls. He envisioned a canal connecting the upper and lower Niagara River that would power a hydroelectric plant to generate electricity for the homes. Digging began in 1890. Mainly due to new innovations in generating electricity, the partially constructed Love Canal was abandoned in 1910. Only a big ditch remained.

Tragically, the ditch was used as a landfill for toxic wastes. The Hooker Chemical Company dumped 21,000 tons of chemicals into the hole. In the 1950s, the company covered the dump and sold the property to the city of Niagara Falls. As new houses and schools sprang up in the area, the population grew to over 85,000 people.

But over time, toxic waste seeped into the soil and into the foundations of people's homes. Contaminated puddles pooled everywhere: in yards, basements, and at schools. A faint, choking smell filled the air. By the late 1970s, 239 families living closest to the canal were forced to evacuate from the area or agreed to move out. Many more protested angrily as more and more children got sick, people died, and babies were born with birth defects.

Notable Quotable

"Quite simply, Love Canal is one of the most appalling environmental tragedies in American history."
—*Eckardt C. Beck, former Environmental Protection Agency (EPA) administrator, 1979.*

EXTREME ENGINEERING

Have you soared through waves on a **flume** ride? The U.S. Army Engineer Research and Development Center depends on its flume to discover cold, hard facts. Army engineers use it for ice research!

The flume is housed at the Cold Regions Research and Engineering Laboratory in Hanover, New Hampshire (CRREL). It's a channel 120 feet long, 4 feet wide, and 2 feet deep (37 meters long, 1.2 meters wide, and over ½ meter deep), used to model solutions to river ice problems. Engineers research different conditions, regulating temperatures down to -20 degrees Fahrenheit (-29 degrees Celsius). Altering the channel's slope, they can test ice covers at different angles.

The flume tests ice jams. It researches **frazil**, which are needle-like ice crystals that flow like gallons of frozen lemonade down rivers. Frazil can trigger disasters when it swirls through flowing waters. Spinning frazil traps barges and ships in an icy grip. It clogs channels and locks. Its floods wreak havoc on communities and businesses.

WORDS to KNOW

flume: an artificial waterway or chute used to study water and **sediment** movement. Also a **gorge** with a stream running through it.

sediment: loose rock particles, such as sand or clay.

gorge: a narrow steep-walled passage through land.

frazil: needle-like ice that forms plates in rapidly flowing water.

Simulate Polluted Waters

SUPPLIES: *clear plastic rectangular tub, water, 4 cotton balls to represent living things, wooden spoon, tweezers, aluminum foil, green food coloring, red food coloring, ¼ cup cooking oil (60 milliliters)*

During Hurricane Katrina, levees were breached and polluted water gushed everywhere. Simulate ways in which toxins can mingle in water.

1 Fill the plastic tub about halfway with water. Place 2 cotton balls in the water to represent living things that thrive in water. Submerge them with the wooden spoon for a moment, then remove the cotton balls with tweezers. Place them on the foil and study them. Apart from making them wet, how has water changed them?

2 Now predict what will happen when you add toxins to clean water. Add several drops of green food coloring to represent herbicides, which are used to kill weeds. Observe what happens. Does the green color stand still or spread? Does it fade and disappear?

3 Predict what will happen when you add red food coloring to the water. Add several drops to represent pesticides, which are used to kill bugs and other pests. Observe what takes place. Do the colors mingle? How does the water source change?

4 Predict how water will change when you add oil. Add oil to represent factory waste. Stir it with the spoon. Does oil blend with the water? How does the water's consistency change?

5 Submerge the remaining cotton balls with the spoon. After a moment, remove them with tweezers. Place them on the foil, and observe them closely. How has the polluted water impacted them? How do these cotton balls differ from the two you submerged in clean water? What conclusions can you draw about how toxins can enter water sources and impact living things?

Compare Piling Foundations

SUPPLIES: *3 small plastic cups of identical size, sand, water, soil, aquarium gravel, modeling clay, 3 craft sticks*

To construct canals, workers drive immense steel pilings deep into the ground for strength and stability. When you drive mini pilings into different soil foundations, you can compare how they hold up.

1 Use cups to construct three different types of foundation soils. Fill the first about one-third of the way with sand. Pour a bit of water into the sand to achieve a soggy consistency.

2 Fill the second cup about one-third of the way with soil. Tamp down on the soil with your fingers to compact it.

3 Combine gravel and clay in the third cup. Press the mixture tightly against the bottom and sides of the cup.

4 Predict how a mini piling will stand up in each foundation. Which foundation will offer the most stability? Will any foundation fail? Test your predictions. Insert one craft stick straight down into each cup so they are all upright. Allow these mini pilings to stand for about 10 minutes. When the time elapses, observe the pilings. Have they shifted or changed?

5 Pour a bit of water into each cup. Allow the cups to stand for another 10 minutes. How are the pilings impacted by the water? What conclusions can you draw about foundation types and stability?

Ice Jam!

SUPPLIES: *aluminum cake tin, pitcher of water, ice cubes, ice chips, freezer*

In some areas, ice jams are an annual spring event. When warmer temperatures and pelting rains cause snow to melt quickly, frozen rivers swell and their waters rise rapidly. The river's top, icy layer ruptures into mammoth chunks of ice that float downstream and obliterate anything in their path. The ice clogs narrow passages in canals and dams, causing their rising waters to create temporary lakes and launch catastrophic flooding. In this experiment, you'll simulate an ice jam.

1 The tin represents a partially frozen river. Pour in a ½ inch layer of water (6.35 millimeters) to represent a slow spring thaw.

2 Jam the river! Place ice cubes and ice chips in the tin. Test to make sure they aren't packed too tightly. Shake the tin. Some ice should move in the water.

3 Place the tin in the freezer. After the water thoroughly freezes, remove the tin.

4 Predict what will happen when you pour water over the ice. Will water flow? Will ice melt? Will cubes and chips respond differently? How long will it take for changes to occur?

5 Carefully shake the tin. What do you observe? You probably notice larger ice chunks remain stuck to the bottom. What changes occurred? Have ice patches broken away? How accurate were your predictions?

6 Predict whether water will flow through the jam. Test your prediction. Hold the tin on an incline above a sink, or prop it up with several books. Pour water from the pitcher. What happens?

Take the Water Flow Challenge

SUPPLIES: *nail, gallon size plastic milk jug, permanent marker, regular plastic straw, sink or tub, pitcher of tap water, stopwatch, jumbo plastic straw, long tubular pasta, duct tape*

Pipes are often used to carry water from canals to where it is needed. A pipe might connect a canal to an underground water system in a city, or to an agricultural area for irrigation. If a pipe bursts it can leave people without water. Experiment with different sizes of pipes to see how they impact flow.
HINT: You'll need an extra pair of hands! Team with a partner. Ask an adult to help you with the nail.

1 Poke a hole near the bottom of the jug. Draw a line halfway up the side of the jug to mark a fill point.

2 Test each "pipe." Insert the regular straw into the hole by carefully enlarging the opening and wriggling the straw into the opening for a snug fit. Stand the jug at the edge of the sink or tub with the straw over the edge. Cover the opening of the straw with your finger while your partner pours water into the jug up to the fill point. Predict what will happen when you allow water to flow.

3 Release your finger and have your partner time the experiment with the stopwatch. How long does it take for the water to flow from the jug?

4 Repeat with the jumbo straw and tubular pasta. Enlarge the opening as necessary. If your pipes distort the hole too much, cover it with duct tape and poke a new hole.

5 How do the results compare? Did you notice the pressure doesn't change with diameter? According to Pascal's Law, pressure applied to a fluid system at rest is felt throughout the system. Water system pressure is the same—no matter what size the pipe is. But when you increase a pipe's size, the water flows more slowly.

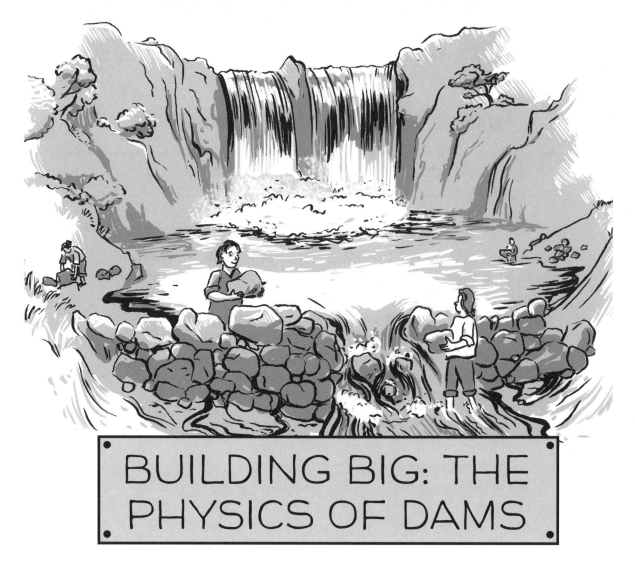

BUILDING BIG: THE PHYSICS OF DAMS

THERE ARE 82,000 DAMS IN THE UNITED STATES ALONE.
Dams are man-made structures that hold back moving water.
Why do we need these huge water barriers? To make sure we
have the right amount of water in the right place at the right
time. Long periods without rain can cause rivers to dry up.

Dams holding back some of the river's water create reservoirs of water
to use during periods of **drought**. The water collected and stored in
reservoirs is used for clean drinking water, irrigation, hydroelectricity,
and flood control. Without these complex structures, many of today's
sprawling cities in the western United States would not exist.

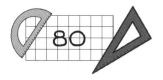

WORDS to KNOW

drought: a long period of time without rain.

wetland: a low area filled with water such as a marsh or swamp.

Dams enabled engineers to bring freshwater and electricity to places like Los Angeles, San Diego, Salt Lake City, Denver, and Phoenix that once seemed impossible to reach. Unfortunately, people didn't always consider the environmental impact of early dams, which can erode waterways and destroy entire habitats.

TROUBLED WATERS

DID YOU KNOW?

Some reservoirs, including Massachusetts' Quabbin Reservoir and California's San Pablo Reservoir, provide recreation areas for fishing, picnicking, and paddling kayaks and canoes.

For 6 million years, the Colorado River has flowed south nearly 1,500 miles from its source high in the Rocky Mountains (2,414 kilometers). According to *Smithsonian* magazine, it traveled "over falls, through deserts and canyons, to the lush **wetlands** of a vast delta in Mexico and into the Gulf of California." But something has changed the course of the river and altered its riverbed. That something is over 100 dams.

Nicknamed the Nile of North America, the Colorado River provides water to many West Coast cities. More than 30 million people depend on it! Today, 1,000 miles of canals cut through the river (1,609 kilometers) and 100 dams block its way. The once-mighty river no longer flows to the sea.

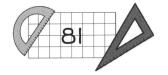

The ecosystem that was once lush and fertile has shrunk to mucky dribbles in Mexico's cracked Sonoran Desert.

The Colorado River isn't the only river in trouble. The Columbia River, once the largest in the Pacific Northwest, was the planet's prime salmon environment. Today, 100 **species** of salmon are extinct and more are threatened. Dams block their way to **spawning habitats**.

WORDS to KNOW

species: a group of living things that are closely related and look the same.

spawning habitat: where an animal goes to lay its eggs.

reservation: an area of land reserved for use by a particular Native American group.

DID YOU KNOW?

The Glen Canyon Dam in Arizona was built right on a Navajo **reservation**, changing the way people had lived off the land for hundreds and hundreds of years. Between 1986 and 1993, 300 large dams worldwide displaced about 4 million people each year.

Because of the environmental destruction caused by dams, many countries, including the United States, no longer build them. But others, such as China, India, and Brazil, are still building dams.

THE PHYSICS OF MAN-MADE DAMS

Engineers ask critical questions in their work to build dams that are stable. How do we block a rushing river? How can we anchor a solid structure in spongy ground? How will the dam stand up to floods and earthquakes?

82

Water is heavy! It weighs 62.4 pounds per cubic foot (999 kilograms per cubic meter). As depth increases, so does **hydrostatic pressure**. At 10 feet deep, (3 meters), water pressure is 10 times greater than at the surface. That's 624 pounds of pressure per cubic foot that a dam would have to resist to remain stable (9,999 cubic kilograms per cubic meter). Beneath the dam's surface, flowing water slams sand and rock into the earth, gnawing away at the soil. And little by little, water seeps into the concrete, slowly weakening the structure.

WORDS to KNOW

hydrostatic pressure: pressure from a liquid's weight.

peat: a mossy soil-like material made of rotting plant matter.

NATURAL DAMS

There are many ways a natural dam can form. When earthquakes, avalanches, and sand floods launch landslides, they dump trails of rock and debris. This can form a natural dam like the one left behind in Spirit Lake, Washington, after Mount St. Helens erupted in 1980. Squishy, spongy **peat** builds up over thousands of years. A peat debris slide can create a natural water obstruction, such as the one that produced a dam in Ireland's Addergoole Bog Lake in 1788. Even jams of logs and vegetation can block water's flow.

At Lassen Volcanic National Park in California, a large lava flow from Cinder Cone volcano is known as the Fantastic Lava Beds. It spilled into river valleys sometime in the 1600s and 1700s when the volcano erupted. When it cooled and hardened, the obstruction created two large lakes, Snag Lake and Butte Lake.

Notable Quotable

"Every successful structure serves as a guide in the construction of all future similar works. Thus the experience of one may become the wisdom of many."

—DeVolson Wood, American civil engineer, 1882

FOUR TYPES OF DAMS

Today engineers have models and computers to figure out how much water a dam must hold back. They also need to consider the dam's purpose and the site's characteristics.

Engineers are always asking questions. How can the dam resist erosion? Will the structure support the water's force? They calculate the necessary size and strength, and based on location and need, engineers choose between four types of dams.

ARCH DAMS: Slim spaces often call for arch dams. These are used in a rocky environment with steep canyons or a narrow gorge. An arch dam is a solid curve. Picture a wall of concrete shaped like a gently sloped letter C curving upstream.

DID YOU KNOW?

A dam has to be built to release controlled quantities of water. It can't stop water completely because the reservoir behind it would fill and water would gush over its top.

BUILDING BIG: THE PHYSICS OF DAMS

DID YOU KNOW?

The Glanun Dam in Saint-Rémy-de-Provence, France, is the world's earliest arch dam. Archaeologists believe Roman engineers constructed it more than 2,000 years ago to supply water to the Roman town of Glanun.

Arch dams are thin, using fewer building materials than other dams. Pressure from water pushing against the arch compresses the concrete. This spreads the weight of the load along the curve to the **abutments** at each end of the arch.

BUTTRESS DAMS: A yawning valley or area of little solid rock is the environment for a **buttress** dam. The front of the dam is a sloping wall that leans slightly downstream. A series of buttresses along the back, shaped like triangles, brace the wall. Water pushes against the wall and the rigid buttresses push back. At the same time, the weight of the dam pushes down into the ground to keep it stable.

WORDS to KNOW

abutment: a structure at the end of an arch that supports its sideways pressure.

buttress: a support built against a wall.

85

EMBANKMENT DAMS: There are more embankment dams than any other type of dam in the United States. An embankment dam is a mammoth mountain of earth, clay, sand, and stone that stands on the solid rock beneath the soil. Through the middle of the mound is a waterproof core of clay. The only thing keeping this dam stable against the strength of a river is its own massive weight. The pyramid shape helps, too. A wide base keeps it steady. Water presses against the walls and the heavy weight of the dam presses down into the ground. Slanted walls send some of the pressure up toward a narrower top and in toward the bulkier, weightier middle.

DID YOU KNOW?

The only man-made structure on Earth bigger than the largest dams is the Great Wall of China. The wall measures 13,170 miles (21,196 kilometers)!

GRAVITY DAMS: Wide valleys often call for gravity dams. These hefty structures are built of tons of expensive concrete. The force of gravity alone keeps them in place. These dams are just too heavy for the sideways push of water to overcome the strength of the downward pull of gravity on the concrete.

BEAVER POWER

Beavers are industrious engineers that use their instincts to build natural embankment dams. They control their pooled-up water to flood areas for protection from **predators** such as bears, bobcats, and coyotes.

When water pools, it's time to build a house. Beavers build their lodges from bottom to top, which means starting underwater. Amphibious beavers are adapted for working beneath the surface. Their large lungs provide plenty of air capacity. They have muscles that seal their ears shut and see-through eyelids like natural goggles. When they clamp their mouths around sticks underwater, skin flaps behind their teeth keep water from gushing in.

WORDS to KNOW

predator: an animal that hunts another animal for food.

incisor: a narrow-edged front tooth used for cutting or gnawing.

Beavers are lumberjacks balancing on paddle-shaped tails. With self-sharpening **incisors** shaped for cutting, they gnaw down trees. They gather branches and sticks, and peel them like bananas to use as building materials. First they plant sticks directly into the bottoms of rivers, lakes, streams, marshes, and ponds. Then they support the sticks with stones, rocks, and chunks of vegetation. After heaping branches and sticks into a domed pile, they use mud to glue wood chunks together for a sturdy coating.

Beavers engineer at least two tunnels into the lodge below the surface of the water for entering, exiting, and fleeing predators. Just above water level is a chamber where beavers dry off and eat. Beavers sleep and take care of their babies in a second chamber just above that. They hide a food stash of logs and branches underwater that lasts all winter.

87

Build a Beaver Dam

SUPPLIES: *paper and pencil, twigs, sticks, bark, wood chips, rocks, mud, grass, reeds, leaves, plastic tub, water, 2 large stones, modeling clay*

Beavers are nature's architects, engineers, and wetland conservationists! These animals change the environment. Use materials found in nature to build a mini dam. Beavers grab any available building materials—even sneakers!
HINT: This is messy, so construct it outdoors.

1 Plan your structure. It should include a platform, tunnels, and a dome-shaped lodge. Use paper and pencil to design a dam.

2 Gather items found in nature for building materials.

3 Depending on how deep the tub is, fill it with 2 to 4 inches of water (5 to 10 centimeters). Place stones inside at opposite ends to anchor the dam. With modeling clay, reinforce the stones.

Notable Quotable

"Anything's possible if you've got enough nerve."
—*J.K. Rowling, creator of the Harry Potter series*

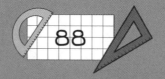

Beavers' front teeth never stop growing! They just get filed down as they chomp up wood. Beavers can gnaw through a 6-inch tree in 15 minutes (15 centimeters).

4 Build a platform with twigs, sticks, bark, wood chips, and rocks. How will it hold together? Will mud be a good material to hold it all together?

5 Build at least two ways for beavers to duck in and out of the lodge. Beavers need to be able to freely swim in and out of the tunnels.

6 Build the lodge. Use heaps of twigs, sticks, grasses, reeds, and leaves. How can you hold it all together, keeping tunnels clear and open?

7 Assess your completed dam. How can you make design modifications for a more successful structure? What other building materials can you use?

TRY THIS

Google it! Google Earth and satellite imagery revealed the planet's largest beaver dam in 2007. Located in Wood Buffalo National Park, Alberta, Canada, it can be seen from space. The dam spans about 2,800 feet (850 meters)! The epic structure was built by several generations of a beaver family beginning in the 1970s—and they're still building! You can go on the Internet to see this dam for yourself. Can you look at other natural and man-made dams on Google Earth?

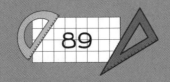

Build an Arch Dam

SUPPLIES: *bread pan, modeling clay, sand, mud, gravel, butter knife, pitcher of water*

Arch dams are suited to span narrow gorges in solid rocky environments. Use trial and error to construct an arch dam. Will your canyon walls support it?

1 Position the bread pan lengthwise. With modeling clay, sand, mud, and gravel, form a narrow canyon down the middle of the pan. Use trial and error to find the best consistency for your building materials. They should be wet enough to be pliable, but they shouldn't be waterlogged, or the canyon will collapse.

2 With the butter knife, carve a notch, or V-shaped groove, across the middle of each of the canyon walls. These are "keyways," where the ends of the arch will attach. If the canyon walls start to slip, find a way to secure them.

3 With the clay, form a solid, curved arch. Make the bottom thicker and heavier than the top. Slide the dam into the notches on either side for support.

4 Predict whether your dam will hold back water. Test it out! Slowly pour water into the reservoir behind the arch. Fill the reservoir as high as it will go without overtopping. Does the dam hold up?

TRY THIS

How will your results be different if you allow the dam to dry overnight before adding water? Predict what will happen. Then test your prediction and compare results.

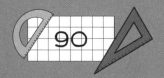

Velocity Curiosity

SUPPLIES: *permanent marker, 3 large foam cups (at least 16 ounces), sharp pencil, masking tape, bathtub or ledge, water, yardstick or tape measure, paper*

Liquid in motion, like a flowing river, produces force and pressure. Pressure is force against a surface. Hydrostatic pressure is force exerted by liquid, which occurs because of gravity. You've learned that the deeper the water, the greater the pressure. Explore how this affects the flow of escaping water from different heights.

1 Mark three pieces of tape with a 1, 2, or 3 with the marker. Label the cups 1, 2, and 3. Use the pencil to poke a hole at different heights in each cup. Predict from which hole the water will have the greatest force as it flows out.

2 Stand the first cup at the side of a bathtub, or outside on a ledge or table. Place your finger over the hole and fill the cup with water.

3 Remove your finger. Observe the water's spout. Place the masking tape numbered 1 at the water's landing point. Measure the distance from the cup. Note it on the paper.

4 Repeat using the other cups. Make a graph that shows how far water traveled from the cups. Compare the results. Which had the most force? What conclusions do you draw?

TRY THIS

> Try using an empty milk carton. Make three holes at varying heights. Tape over the holes, fill with water, then remove the tape to test the water flow.

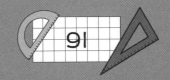

Tsunami!

SUPPLIES: *clear plastic tub, water, table, piece of wood the width of the plastic tub, paper and pencil, stopwatch, measuring tape*

An underwater earthquake can trigger a tsunami. The mammoth waves of tsunamis move with a tremendous force that can destroy a dam. Make your own wave tank to simulate a tsunami. HINT: This is messy! Try it outside.

1 Fill the tub 2 inches deep with water (5 centimeters). Place it in the center of the table. Allow the water to calm before the next step.

2 At a narrow end of the tub, press the wood into the water. Move it slowly against the water to create a low, flat wave. Use trial and error to generate a series of strong, steady waves. Practice until you can create uniform waves.

3 Observe the waves' action inside the tub. Sketch a diagram of what you observe.

4 Allow the water to calm. This time, use the stopwatch to time how long it takes waves to travel from the edge of the wood to the opposite end of the tub. Record the time.

5 Now vary the water depth. What are your results in 1 inch of water (2½ centimeters)? In 1½ inches (4 centimeters)? In 3 inches? What conclusions can you draw about what happens to tsunami waves as they approach the shore?

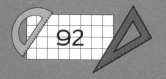

AMAZING DAMS

WHETHER YOU'RE LOOKING AT AN ANCIENT MAYA STONE DAM in Guatemala or a massive concrete structure in Russia, the sight of a giant dam construction is startling. Dams are some of the world's most impressive feats of innovation and engineering.

SADD-EL-KAFARA DAM: NILE RIVER, ANCIENT EGYPT

- **TYPE:** embankment dam with stone
- **PURPOSE:** drinking water
- **CONSTRUCTION DATE:** about 2700 BCE

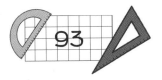

More than 4,000 years ago, the ancient Egyptians attempted to tame the water of the mighty Nile River by engineering one of civilization's earliest dams. For about 15 years, laborers toiled in the sweltering heat of the cracked desert sand to construct a dam of rough stone. They built a colossal structure about 350 feet long (107 meters) and 37 feet high (11 meters). About 60,000 tons of gravel, stone, and rubble filled its pyramid shape, while mounds more surrounded it. But history's earliest recorded dam was demolished without ever being used!

Notable Quotable

"Life is trying things to see if they work."
—*Ray Bradbury, legendary sci-fi author, poet, and playwright*

WORDS to KNOW

spillway: a channel for an overflow of water.

Sadd-el-Kafara Dam's engineers probably thought the structure was sturdy. Unfortunately, it had a fatal design flaw. It lacked a **spillway**. There was no channel or tunnel to carry the river around the dam site while it was being built.

When an unexpected flood occurred during construction, the dam was destroyed by the same water it was supposed to control. Without a spillway, the water crashed over the dam, destroying everything in its path. The core crumbled like a gigantic graham cracker. The top of the dam wasn't yet finished and overtopping eroded it. Ancient engineers turned away from dam building and it would be thousands of years before they tried again.

ASWAN HIGH DAM:
NILE RIVER, ASWAN, EGYPT

- **TYPE:** embankment dam
- **PURPOSE:** flood control, irrigation, electricity, support fishing
- **CONSTRUCTION DATE:** completed in 1970

WORDS to KNOW

antiquity: something from ancient times.

UNESCO World Heritage Site: a place considered to be of special cultural or physical significance by the United Nations Educations, Scientific and Cultural Organization (UNESCO).

In 1960, Egyptian engineers were back in action constructing the Aswan Dam to harness the Nile's waters to generate hydroelectricity. Engineers faced a monumental challenge. The dam's reservoir would submerge much of the region of Lower Nubia. This included the precious **antiquities** and monuments at the Abu Simbel temple complex. It would sink important archeological sites and destroy **UNESCO World Heritage Sites**.

How could engineers preserve the past,
while building the future?

Teams from around the world joined the efforts.

Spain, Italy, the Netherlands, and the United States played important roles. Surveyors studied the area. People joined to excavate the archaeological sites. Workers dismantled endangered antiquities, cutting apart and carving up monuments. Laborers hauled sections of monuments to another safe site where they reassembled them! It proved a wonder of ingenuity.

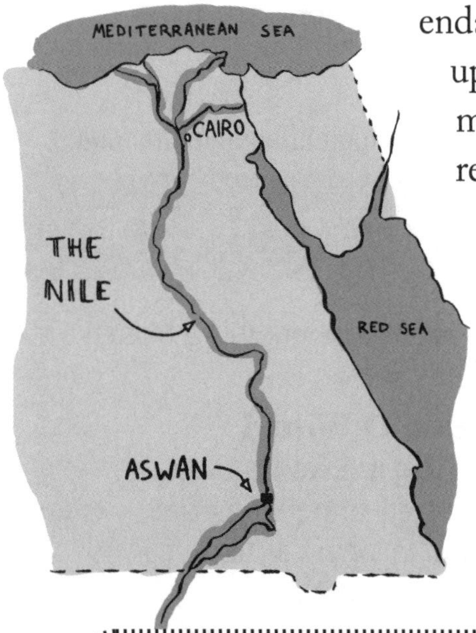

The Aswan Dam is 12,533 feet long (3,820 meters) and 364 feet tall (111 meters). It supplies about half of Egypt's power. At its fastest, 388,000 cubic feet of water can pass through the dam in one second (11,000 cubic meters). Construction of the dam is considered the twentieth century's greatest feat of engineering. For the first time in history the unpredictable Nile River was tamed. Unfortunately, in the process, 90,000 Nubians were moved from their homes and relocated.

(Map labels: MEDITERRANEAN SEA, CAIRO, THE NILE, RED SEA, ASWAN)

WORDS to KNOW

petroglyph: a rock carving.

DID YOU KNOW?

Today, Pakistan's Diamer-Basha Dam is under construction. It will be important for irrigation, drinking water, and electricity. However, it will displace about 33,000 ancient **petroglyphs**. Some are over 10,000 years old. Museums will house and protect the priceless antiquities.

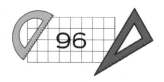

HOOVER DAM: BORDER OF ARIZONA AND NEVADA, UNITED STATES

- **TYPE:** concrete arch-gravity dam
- **PURPOSE:** flood control, irrigation, hydroelectric power
- **CONSTRUCTION DATES:** 1931–1936

In the Southwest, cycles of drought and floods on the Colorado River posed constant concerns. During the **Great Depression**, the United States built a dam to span the remote Black Canyon and hold back the unpredictable river. Building the dam would provide jobs for an eager work force. It would provide water and hydroelectricity so that new cities, such as Los Angeles and Las Vegas, could grow and flourish.

WORDS to KNOW

Great Depression: a 10-year period of a severe worldwide economic downturn.

The Hoover Dam is an arch-gravity dam. Engineers designed the curved structure to use properties of the arch. Water's weight pushes along the arch's curve and Black Canyon's walls push back.

The water squishes, or compresses, the concrete in the arch. Through compression, the dam is extremely stiff.

CONCRETE COLOSSUS

The Hoover Dam's 6,600,000 tons of waterproof concrete, is heavy enough that water's tremendous weight can't crush it or knock it down. In fact, it's so heavy that it didn't even need to be curved!

The Hoover Dam is one of the largest concrete structures ever built. It soars more than 700 feet above **bedrock** (213 meters) over Black Canyon. Builders poured over 3.3 million cubic yards of concrete in construction (2.5 million cubic meters). That's enough to build a 4-foot-wide sidewalk around the earth at the equator (1.2 meters wide)! The dam is a popular tourist attraction and landmark, hosting nearly 3 million visitors a year.

WORDS to KNOW

bedrock: solid rock under soil.
hazardous: extremely dangerous.

GRUELING LABOR

In 1935, President Franklin Delano Roosevelt launched the dam in an official ceremony. He called it "a symbol of an American spirit." During the tough times of the Great Depression, construction of the Hoover Dam provided much-needed jobs. A total of 21,000 men worked on the Hoover Dam. But they worked in a **hazardous** environment of very hot temperatures.

After laying a foundation and building cofferdams, workers risked their lives at staggering heights. They scaled Black Canyon's rocky walls and perched on scrawny 1-foot by 2-foot wooden seats (30 by 60 centimeters). Laborers shimmied down ropes, hoisting 45-pound jackhammers. They blasted into rock with dynamite, all the while dangling on ropes. Yawning beneath them was a vast open space! Adding to the risks was constant uncertainty. High climbers never knew exactly what would tumble off the canyon. It might be the entire rock wall!

Deep in the belly of the earth, laborers blasted tunnels as wide as four-lane freeways. They diverted the river. Workers roasted underground as temperatures sizzled above 130 degrees Fahrenheit (55 degrees Celsius). In one month, during the sweltering summer of 1941, 14 people died from heat stroke.

DID YOU KNOW?

A myth . . . busted! For years, people claimed that workers were accidentally buried inside the Hoover Dam as concrete was poured, but this is not true. The official number of construction fatalities from the Bureau of Reclamation is 96. Workers tragically and often suddenly died. The first fatalities happened even before construction when two men drowned surveying the dam. Some workers received fatal injuries during blasting. Others were crushed in rockslides or tumbled off cliff walls to their deaths. A plaque at Hoover Dam honors the dead. "They died to make the desert bloom."

HYDRO POWER

How does the Hoover Dam produce hydroelectric power? With powerful velocity, flowing water falls into intake pipes. It flows downstream through the pipes into massive **turbine** blades where the water spins the blades at high speeds. Spinning turbines turn an upright shaft that connects with a **generator**. Inside, a **rotor** shaped like a wheel and filled with magnets spins along copper wires. The twirling magnets generate electricity, which travels along the wires and out of the dam. Hoover Dam's 17 generators produce 4 billion kilowatt hours of hydroelectric power for over a million people in California, Arizona, and Nevada.

WORDS to KNOW

turbine: a machines that use water or steam to produce motion.

generator: a machine that turns energy in motion into electricity.

rotor: the rotating part of a generator.

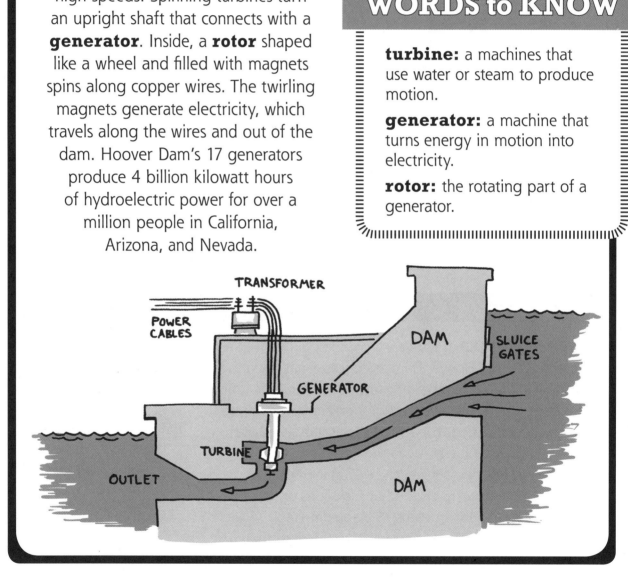

AMAZING DAMS ACROSS THE GLOBE

ITAIPÚ DAM (Paraná River, Brazil and Paraguay, 1975–1991)

- Built to generate hydroelectricity, the Itaipú Dam is 25,980 feet long (7,919 meters) and 363 feet high (196 meters).

- Engineers changed the course of the Paraná River to build this dam! This is the world's largest hydroelectric plant, as tall as a towering 65-story skyscraper. In 2000, the hollow concrete gravity dam produced 93,428 gigawatt hours (GWh) of power. A world record!

ROBERT-BOURASSA DAM (La Grande River, Quebec, Canada, 1974–1981)

- Built to generate hydroelectricity, Robert-Bourassa Dam is 9,301 feet long (2,835 meters) and 351 feet high (162 meters).

- This embankment dam is nicknamed "a giant's staircase." Its spillway features 10 steps, each the size of two football fields.

- North America's largest generating site blasts 7,722 megawatts of power. It's also the world's largest underground dam, plunging 459 feet beneath solid bedrock (140 meters).

DID YOU KNOW?

Extreme engineering, extreme sports! The Contra Dam towers over the Verazasc River along Italy's border in Ticono, Switzerland. The concrete arch dam is known for its slim, elegant design. Its heart-stopping 722-foot bungee drop (220 meters) was featured in the James Bond film *Golden Eye*. Some film buffs consider it the best stunt ever!

SAND DAMS (Kipsing, Kenya, 1995–ongoing)

- Typically 164 feet long (50 meters) and between 3 and 16 feet high (1 to 5 meters), sand dams are built to provide irrigation and drinking water.

- Built with reinforced concrete over temporary, sandy rivers, cost-efficient sand dams capture precious water that falls during the short rainy seasons. They store the resource to be used during the dry season.

THREE GORGES DAM (Yangtze River, China, 1994–2006)

- The Three Gorges Dam is 6,500 feet long (1,980 meters) and 600 feet high (185 meters). It was built for flood control, hydroelectric power, and navigation.

- This is the world's largest hydroelectric project and single largest source of electrical power.

- The $23 billion dam is one of the world's most controversial structures. It displaced 1.13 million people and wiped out the Yangtze River dolphin's habitat, pushing the animal to extinction in 2007.

- The dam also impacted the area's weather! Scientists believe it increased rainfall and lowered temperatures.

Marshmallow Arch

SUPPLIES: *paper and pencil, measuring tape, toothpicks, mini marshmallows*

The Hoover Dam uses properties of the arch. Use only mini marshmallows, toothpicks, and trial and error to construct an arch that resists collapse.

1 Identify the problem you need to solve. Ask questions as you think through your plan and design your arch. On what kind of base will the arch stand? Where will the toothpicks and marshmallows connect? How will you join the arch at the curved center? Use paper and pencil to sketch the structure, noting planned dimensions.

2 Will you build the arch on its side in a flat position and then stand it up, or construct it in a standing position? Follow your design. Build the sides first, starting at the bottom. Build parallel, horizontal rows of marshmallows. Be sure each row uses the same number. Connect marshmallows with toothpicks to hold the structure in place. Trial and error will help you figure out the best method.

3 Work your way up the sides until you reach the area where the arch forms. How will you curve the structure? Locate the arch's center. How will you connect the two sides?

4 Does your arch stand or collapse? Where is it weak? How can you modify plans for a sturdier structure?

TRY THIS

With only marshmallows, can you build an arch that stays standing?

Timber Dam

SUPPLIES: *garden trowel, large plastic tub, sand, toy buildings, toy trees or plant cuttings, toy people and animals, craft sticks, rocks and gravel, pail of water*

Early dams in the United States were built of timber. Can you build a structurally sound dam out of wood that stops water flow? HINT: This is messy! Try it outside!

1 Use the trowel to fill the tub with sand. Carve a river and pack the sand tightly against the carved area to reinforce it. Add toy houses and other buildings to represent people and businesses that will depend on the dam. Add toy trees or plant cuttings to represent plants that depend on the habitat. Position the toy people and animals.

2 Decide where to construct a dam. Consider the town. How can you avoid displacing people and destroying habitats? Consider the structure. Where will the greatest amount of water pressure push the dam? What shape will best handle the pressure?

3 Construct the dam with craft sticks to represent timber. Use sand to hold the timbers together. Reinforce the dam with rocks and gravel.

4 Fill the river! Slowly pour a small amount of water from the pail into the carved-out area. Does the shape hold up? Does water pass through the dam? Add more water, pouring faster. Does the dam hold it, or does the structure fail?

5 Go back to the drawing board, and try again. Will a different shape work better? Modify and improve the design.

TRY THIS

Spending a day at the beach? Construct a sand dam offshore. Will it keep back water?

Whoa, Water Flow!

SUPPLIES: *paint tray, 2 buckets of sand, garden trowel, toy buildings and trees, paper and pencil, building materials (clay, rocks, stones, and gravel, craft sticks, sponges, twigs, drinking straws, rubber bands), protractor, 3 blocks of wood (6 inches or 15 centimeters each), 2-liter bottle filled with tap water, bucket*

Simulate a flood with a stream table. Then design and construct a dam to see if it will hold back floodwaters. HINT: Ask an adult to make a quarter-sized hole in the bottom of the tray so water can drain out into a bucket.

1 Fill the paint tray with sand. Use the trowel to carve a winding river that is ½-inch deep (1¼ centimeters). Set up houses, schools, and other buildings along the riverbanks to represent a community that depends on the river.

2 Design and build a dam over the river's path. Where will you place it? How will you use the building materials? Sketch out your plans, then use the various building materials to build the dam.

3 Set up the stream table. Use the protractor to set the wood blocks and paint tray at a 5-degree angle. Position the bucket under the small hole in the stream table. Will water wash away the sand? Will the dam stand up? Will it stop water's flow? Predict what will happen.

4 Slowly fill the riverbed with water from the bottle. Does the dam hold up? Is the community impacted?

5 Imagine that a substantial, sudden rainfall floods the community. Quickly dump the rest of the water into the river. Does your dam resist failure? How is the community impacted?

6 Modify your design and building materials to create a more substantial dam. Test your dam at different angles to change the strength of the water flow.

Treat Raw Water

SUPPLIES: *bucket, garden trowel, measuring cups, 2½ cups mud and dirt, water, funnel, 2-liter plastic bottles (1 with cap, 2 with the top cut off, and 1 with the bottom cut off), water pitcher, 2 tablespoons alum, clean coffee filter, rubber band, 1 cup gravel, 1½ cups coarse sand, 1½ cups fine sand, large wooden spoon, timer, paper, pencil*

Some water controlled by dams is used to supply drinking water for nearby communities. Before raw water is safe to drink, it must be treated. HINT: You can find alum in grocery stores. Check the spice aisle. Safely dispose of water after you've completed the activity. It's not safe to drink!

1 To prepare raw water, use the bucket, trowel, and measuring cups to collect 2½ cups of mud and dirt (½ liter). Pour 5 quarts of water into it (5 liters).

2 Place the funnel into the intact bottle's opening. Fill the bottle with raw water. Tightly seal with the cap.

3 Add air to the raw water by shaking the bottle for 30 seconds. Gases trapped in the water escape as you shake. That adds oxygen. To add more air, pour the water back and forth 10 times between the pitcher and the bottle.

FINE SAND

COURSE SAND

GRAVEL

RUBBER BAND

COFFEE FILTER

4 Now pour the aerated water into one bottle with the top cut off. Add alum and slowly stir with the spoon for 5 minutes. Dirt and other suspended solid particles clump together. That makes them easier to filter out for removal at a treatment plant. Do you notice furry clumps of alum and particles? This is called floc.

Notable Quotable

"Never give up; for even rivers someday wash dams away."
—*Arthur Golden, author of* Memoirs of a Geisha.

5 Particles suspended in liquid form sediments. Allow the water to stand for 20 minutes. Check it every 5 minutes. Sketch what you observe. How is it changing? Does gravity pull the floc down? Where does the material settle?

6 Make a filter using the bottle with the bottom cut off. Wrap the coffee filter around the neck. Secure it with the rubber band. Turn the bottle upside down and place it inside the remaining bottle with the top cut off. Pour a layer of gravel into the filter bottle, a layer of coarse sand over the gravel, and then a layer of fine sand. Carefully, without disturbing the top layer, pour 3 quarts of water through the filter (3 liters). That cleans the water.

7 After a large amount of sediment collects in the bottle of raw water, observe filtration by pouring about two-thirds of it into the filter. Compare the filtered water with the remaining raw water. What do you observe? Sketch and label the two samples.

DID YOU KNOW?

The Yellowstone River is the only river in the United States that is longer than 600 miles and not largely altered by dams. But some dams in the United States are being removed. Some are removed because they are old and not worth repairing. Others have been removed because they cause too much environmental damage.

The Edwards Dam in Maine was the first to be removed for environmental reasons. Many fish, like the Atlantic salmon, have since returned to the Kennebec River. By 2020, 85 percent of all the nation's dams will be at least half a century old and many are already in need of repair.

DAM DISASTERS

DAMS DON'T HOLD UP FOREVER.
In time, nature takes its toll. Waters breach them and erode foundations. Broiling and freezing weather cracks them. Gates rust and loosen, and engineering failures happen. Eventually, every dam has to be repaired, removed, or replaced.

ROCKSLIDE! ENGINEERING FAILURE

When an engineering failure occurs in an enormous structure, its impact is also enormous. In 1963, a dam failure occurred in the beautiful Dolomite Mountains region in Italy, 63 miles from Venice (100 kilometers). It was the most devastating landslide in Europe's history.

Vajont Dam was constructed in a steep, narrow gorge in the Vajont River's scenic valley. It's the world's highest thin-arch dam, towering 860 feet above the valley floor (262 meters). The mountains in the area have huge, upright limestone cliffs, while the valleys below them are filled with weaker clay. Did engineers and geologists think enough about rock characteristics when planning the dam? Many believe they did not.

Just two years after construction began, workers noticed slips, shifts, and fractures in the rock. **Disintegrating** rock caused minor landslides. Worried engineers tested the stability of the dam's banks. Three test borings didn't reveal weaknesses so the project moved ahead.

In 1961, engineers first filled the reservoir.

WORDS to KNOW

disintegrate: to break down or decay.

fault: a fracture in a rock formation.

fissure: a narrow split or crack in rock.

DID YOU KNOW?

When Italy's Contra Dam reservoirs were filled, the action launched seismic activities and triggered a series of earthquakes. What caused this? Earth scientists theorize that the weight of the reservoirs stressed **faults**, and pressure from seeping water placed stress on **fissures**.

The water's crushing weight slammed the weak clay layers in the landmass. Banks cracked, and in just 10 minutes over 24 million cubic feet of rock slid into the lake (700,000 cubic meters).

To avoid more landslides, engineers tried to carefully control the level of the lake and the speed of the reservoir's filling. They raised and lowered water levels many times, but the series of reservoir fillings and **drawdowns** triggered another landslide—and this time it wasn't minor.

In late September 1963, engineers lowered the water. Days later, the entire landmass of more than 9 billion cubic feet slipped (260 million cubic meters). The high-velocity landslide went crashing into the reservoir, completely blocking the gorge. With more than 4 trillion cubic feet of water in the reservoir (115 million cubic meters), massive waves overtopped the dam. Crushing water destroyed the village of Casso. Floods spread to other villages and towns in the area. Over 2,000 people died.

WORDS to KNOW

drawdown: lowering a water level.

DID YOU KNOW?

Frightening landslides threaten the banks of China's Three Gorges Dam. Its construction relocated 1.3 million people. Now tens of thousands must move for a second time because of landslides and water pollution.

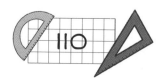

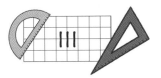

DAM DISASTERS

BOUNCING BOMBS: PLANNED DISASTER

It was May 16, 1943, during World War II, when a group of men from England's air force had to carry out a dangerous job. The "Dambusters" of England's 617 Squadron's Royal Air Force (RAF) soared above Germany in bombers. Their mission was to destroy the reservoirs providing the water that powered Germany's weapons **industry**. Bombing these dams would stop work in Germany's mines and factories and weaken their ability to wage war.

The mission required a feat of engineering. No bomber plane in England could carry a bomb large enough to breach the dams. English engineer, scientist, and inventor Barnes Wallis (1887-1979) figured out that a smaller bomb at the bottom of the dam could do the trick. So he designed the "bouncing bomb." When it was dropped at the right speed, from the right height, and at the right angle, the bouncing bomb skipped across the water, hit the dam, and rolled to the bottom!

WORDS to KNOW

industry: the large-scale production of goods, especially in factories.

To carry out the mission, 19 aircraft took off, flying hazardously low. With amazing precision, bombers pummeled reservoirs with bouncing bombs. Dams splintered and breached. Water flooded farmlands and crushed roads and bridges.

The Dambuster Raid proved a success but the 617 Squadron suffered tragic losses. Three of the planes were shot down on the way to the targets and two were damaged. Three of the remaining planes were lost in the attacks. Of the 133 men who took part in the dangerous raid, only 11 made it back safely. There were 53 men who died and three who were captured by the enemy. After the war, countries agreed not to bomb each other's dams if the power of the water is so strong that it can kill too many innocent **civilians**.

DID YOU KNOW?

In 1881, Clara Barton formed the American Red Cross to help communities after a disaster. The Johnstown flood marked the organization's first peacetime disaster relief efforts when 50 Red Cross volunteers arrived to help the survivors.

WORDS to KNOW

civilian: someone not involved in fighting a war.

neglected: not taken care of.

SOUTH FORK DAM
AND THE JOHNSTOWN FLOOD

In 1889, a wall of rushing water overcame a **neglected** earth dam, nearly destroying Johnstown, Pennsylvania. The South Fork Dam created a recreational lake in the community. But the dam had been patched after springing some leaks and, tragically, it did not hold.

Notable Quotable
"We cannot solve our problems with the same thinking we used when we created them."
—*Albert Einstein*

Rain and snowmelt filled the lake, seeped over the top of the dam, and the structure collapsed. A furious wall of water 40-feet high (12 meters) and half a mile wide (0.8 kilometers) steamrolled through the booming steel and coal town. It caved in homes and buildings.

The debris it carried along was not just a mixture of rocks, dirt, and trees. It included wrecked train cars, dead and injured people and animals, and splintered homes. The more junk it sucked into its mass, the more powerful the wall became, moving at an average speed of 40 miles per hour (64 kilometers per hour). In less than 10 minutes, it destroyed everything in its path.

Over 2,200 people perished in the tragedy. People from all over the country were so moved by the story that they sent money, clothing, food, medicine, bandages, and lumber. Volunteers came to help. In just one month, stores reopened for business.

DAM DEMOLITION

For over 100 years, the Elwha River in Washington's Olympic Peninsula has been cut off from its source. The Elwha and Glines Canyon hydroelectric dams built on the river helped some communities develop and prosper. But they harmed others. Construction flooded the Lower Elwha Klahlam tribe's sacred lands. Spawning habitats for Pacific salmon disappeared and the structure blocked the path of five other species. After damming, the salmon population shriveled in number from 400,000 to 3,000.

In 2011, the United States launched its largest dam-removal project here. It took almost 30 years to work out the details and find the money needed for the job. Glines Canyon Dam is a 210-foot-tall arch (64 meters) and Elwha Dam stood 105 feet high (32 meters). The Elwha Dam is already down and water flows over what is left of Glines Canyon Dam. But enough silt, sand, clay, and rock to fill a football field over 2 miles deep (3 kilometers) built up behind the dams. Its release has to be controlled so it doesn't kill spawning fish. Salmon are already returning and sacred sites that had been submerged by the reservoirs will return to the Lower Elwha Klahlam tribe.

Can you imagine watching the environment transform before your eyes? Robert Young, a geoscientist on the project explains. "We want (kids) to think, 'Maybe science is something I could do. I could be fixing the river. I could be helping it heal. I could be uncovering sacred sites. That could be me. And it should be me.'"

You're the Engineer!

SUPPLIES: *bucket of water, cans, clamps, craft sticks, duct tape, foam egg cartons, glue, gravel, masking tape, modeling clay, paper clips, pencil, plastic milk jugs, plastic tubs, plastic wrap, sand, scissors, sponges, string or twine, toothpicks*

Through innovation, engineers solve problems. Use the engineering design process to create a structure that solves a problem. Base the problem on one in your community, such as aging infrastructure, flooding, or troubles for migratory fish. Or use your imagination to invent a problem. Decide which will better solve the problem, a canal or a dam. Think big! Then build small to make a prototype.

1 **IDENTIFY THE PROBLEM** What do you need to accomplish? Ask questions and gather information. Set your goal.

2 **BRAINSTORM POSSIBLE SOLUTIONS** Write down everything that comes to mind. Afterward, zoom in on the idea with the greatest potential.

3 **DESIGN AND DRAW A PLAN** Draw a diagram and plan for your solution. Choose your tools and building materials.

4 **BUILD THE PROTOTYPE** Notice anything that seems like it won't work.

5 **TEST THE PROTOTYPE** Is it sturdy? Give it a push or a pull. Does it withstand forces and loads? Will it resist collapse?

6 **EVALUATE SUCCESS** What worked well or didn't work with the design? What adjustments will make your structure better? What other tools or materials can you use?

7 **REDESIGN WITH IMPROVEMENTS** Back to the drawing board!

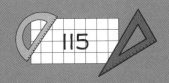

GLOSSARY

abutment: a structure at the end of an arch that supports its sideways pressure.

amphibious: living or working both on land and in water.

ancestors: the people that lived before you.

antiquity: something from ancient times.

aqueduct: a pipe or channel that moves water over long distances.

aquifer: a layer of sand, gravel, and rock that has pores or openings through which groundwater flows.

archaeologist: a scientist who studies ancient people through the objects left behind.

bank: the sloped side of a river.

barge: a boat with a flat bottom used to carry loads on canals and rivers.

BCE: put after a date, BCE stands for Before Common Era and counts down to zero. CE stands for Common Era and counts up from zero. These non-religious terms correspond to BC and AD.

bedrock: solid rock under soil.

boring: making a hole.

breach: to make an opening through something.

brittle: easily broken, cracked, or snapped.

buoyancy: a force that allows an object to float in liquid.

buttress: a support built against a wall.

canal: a man-made waterway built for shipping, navigation, or irrigation.

cargo: things carried by ship.

channel: a long narrow passage or tube along which a liquid can flow.

chemistry: the science of how substances interact, combine, and change.

civilian: someone not involved in fighting a war.

civilization: a community of people that is advanced in art, science, and government.

cofferdam: a temporary watertight structure pumped dry and used for underwater construction.

collapse: to fall in or down suddenly.

compression: a pushing force that squeezes or presses material inward.

counterweight: an equal weight that balances an object.

course: the path a river takes from its source, where it begins, to its mouth, where it empties.

crop: a plant grown for food and other uses.

current: the steady movement of water in a certain direction.

cutting: a small, man-made valley cut through a hill.

dam: a barrier built across a river or stream to control and collect water.

data: information, facts, and numbers from tests and experiments.

dead load: the actual, constant weight of a structure.

dense: how tightly the matter in an object is packed.

disintegrate: to break down or decay.

displace: to force people, animals, or things from their usual place.

displacement: when something is moved by an object taking its place.

downstream: in the direction of a stream's current, away from its source.

drawdown: lowering a water level.

drought: a long period of time without rain.

dynamic load: load that changes over time and is applied through motion.

dynamite: a highly explosive material.

earthquake: a sudden movement in pieces of the outer layer of the earth.

energy: the ability to do work.

engineer: someone who uses science and math to design and build structures such as buildings, bridges, tunnels, canals, and dams.

engineering: using science and math to design and build structures.

environment: everything in nature, living and nonliving, including plants, animals, soil, rocks, and water.

epidemic: an outbreak of a disease that spreads quickly.

equator: the imaginary line around the earth, halfway between the North and South Poles.

equilibrium: the state of balance between opposing forces.

erosion: the gradual wearing away of soil by water or ice.

excavate: to dig out earth and soil.

famine: a severe shortage of food resulting in widespread hunger.

fault: a fracture in a rock formation.

fertile: good for growing crops.

fissure: a narrow split or crack in rock.

floodgate: a gate in a waterway that is used to control the flow of water.

flotilla: a number of vessels.

fluid: a substance such as a gas or a liquid that flows freely and has no fixed shape.

flume: an artificial waterway or chute used to study water and sediment movement. Also a gorge with a stream running through it.

force: a push or pull that changes an object's motion.

frazil: needle-like ice that forms plates in rapidly flowing water.

freshwater: water that is not salty.

friction: the force that resists motion between two objects in contact.

generator: a machine that turns energy in motion into electricity.

geologist: a scientist who studies the earth.

geometric: using straight lines and simple shapes such as circles or squares.

gorge: a narrow steep-walled passage through land.

gravity: a physical force that pulls bodies toward the center of the earth.

Great Depression: a 10-year period of a severe worldwide economic downturn.

groundwater: water located in the ground.

habitat: the natural area where a plant or an animal lives.

hazardous: extremely dangerous.

hydraulic engineering: water control and transportation.

hydraulic press: a machine that uses liquid pressure to exert force on a small piston, which moves a larger piston.

hydroelectricity: electricity generated from water power.

hydrologist: a scientist who studies the earth's water.

hydrostatic pressure: pressure from a liquid's weight.

hypothesis: an unproven idea that tries to explain certain facts or observations.

immigrant: a person who comes to settle in a new country.

incisor: a narrow-edged front tooth used for cutting or gnawing.

inclined plane: an angled surface.

industry: the large-scale production of goods, especially in factories.

infrastructure: public works, such as water and power, that support a community.

ingenuity: being clever, original, and inventive.

innovation: a new way of doing something.

interaction: how things work together.

irrigation: supplying land with water using pipes and ditches, usually for crops.

isthmus: a narrow strip of land bordered by water on both sides, joining two larger land areas.

landslide: the sliding down of a mass of earth or rock from a mountain or cliff.

levee: a wall of earth or stone built along a riverbank to prevent flooding of the land.

lever: a bar that rests on a support and lifts or moves things.

live load: the changing weight of vehicles, pedestrians, and other things that are placed on a structure.

livestock: animals raised for food or other products.

load: an applied force or weight.

lock: a step that allows barges to move up or down a canal.

maize: corn.

malaria: an infectious disease transmitted by mosquito bites.

maritime: related to the sea, sailing, or shipping.

matter: what an object is made of.

natural resource: a material or substance such as gold, wood, and water that occurs in nature and is valuable to humans.

navigable: deep and wide enough for a boat or ship to pass through.

neglected: not taken care of.

nutrients: the substances in food and soil that keep animals and plants healthy and growing.

open-ended: able to adapt to the needs of a situation.

overtop: to rise above the top of a barrier.

parallel: lines extending in the same direction, keeping the same distance between them.

peat: a mossy soil-like material made of rotting plant matter.

petroglyph: a rock carving.

physical science: the study of the physical world.

physics: the science of how matter and energy work together. A physicist studies physics.

pivotal: vitally important.

predator: an animal that hunts another animal for food.

pressure: a force acting on a surface from an object or fluid.

principle: the basic way that something works.

prototype: a working model or mock-up that allows engineers to test their solution.

pyroengineer: to use fire in toolmaking to treat stones.

reservation: an area of land reserved for use by a particular Native American group.

reservoir: an artificial lake or tank for collecting and storing water.

riverbed: the area between the banks of a river ordinarily covered by water.

rotor: the rotating part of a generator.

rupture: to burst or break suddenly.

saturate: to soak with water.

sediment: loose rock particles, such as sand or clay.

seismic: relating to earthquakes.

silt: fine soil rich in nutrients.

sluice gate: a gate that opens to allow water to flow in and out of locks.

solution: an answer to a problem.

spawning habitat: where an animal goes to lay its eggs.

species: a group of living things that are closely related and look the same.

spillway: a channel for an overflow of water.

statics: an area of physics related to forces and the ways they produce equilibrium.

stealth: silent or secret.

structure: a bridge, tunnel, building, dam, or other object built from a number of different parts put together in a certain way.

survey: to use math to measure angles, distances, and elevations on Earth's surfaces.

technical: relating to scientific or mechanical methods.

technological: a way of applying tools and methods to do something.

tension: a pulling force that pulls or stretches material outward.

tetrahedron: a pyramid containing four triangular faces.

theorize: to come up with an idea that explains how or why something happens.

towpath: a path along a river or canal used for towing barges and boats.

toxic: something that is poisonous.

trade: buying and selling goods and services.

trajectory: the curve a body travels along in its path through space.

trapezoid: a four-sided shape with two parallel sides and two non-parallel sides.

trial and error: trying first one thing, then another and another, until something works.

tsunami: an enormous wave formed by a disturbance under the water, like an earthquake or volcano.

tunnel: a passageway that goes through or under natural or man-made obstacles such as rivers, mountains, roads, and buildings.

turbine: a machines that use water or steam to produce motion.

UNESCO World Heritage Site: a place considered to be of special cultural or physical significance by the United Nations Educations, Scientific and Cultural Organization (UNESCO).

upstream: against the direction of a stream's current, toward its source.

vessel: a ship or large boat.

volume: the amount of space inside an object.

water pressure: the pressure exerted by water.

wetland: a low area filled with water such as a marsh or swamp.

BOOKS

Caney, Steven. *Steven Caney's Ultimate Building Book*, Running Press Kids, 2006.

Dutemple, Lesley A. *The Hoover Dam*. Lerner, 2003.

Latham, Donna. *Bridges and Tunnels: Investigate Feats of Engineering*. Nomad Press, 2012.

Levy, Matthys. *Engineering the City: How Infrastructure Works*. Chicago Review Press, 2000.

Salvadori, Mario. *The Art of Construction: Projects and Principles for Beginning Engineers & Architects*. Chicago Review Press, 2000.

Sullivan, George. *Built to Last: Building America's Amazing Bridges, Dams, Tunnels, and Skyscrapers*. Scholastic, 2005.

WEB SITES

American Experience: Hoover Dam
www.pbs.org/wgbh/americanexperience/films/hoover/

American Experience: Panama Canal
www.pbs.org/wgbh/americanexperience/films/panama/player/

EngineerGirl!
www.engineergirl.org/

Discovery Channel: Extreme Engineering
dsc.discovery.com/convergence/engineering/engineering.html

Hoover Dam Factoids for Kids
www.usbr.gov/lc/hooverdam/educate/kidfacts.html

Know the Facts on Flooding from FEMA
www.ready.gov/know-facts

Make the Dirt Fly! (Panama Canal)
www.sil.si.edu/Exhibitions/Make-the-Dirt-Fly/whybuild.html

NOAA: Earth Cam Construction Camera, Rogue River Restoration
www.earthcam.com/clients/noaa/rogueriver/

Nova: Flood!
www.pbs.org/wgbh/nova/flood/

PBS: Building Big
www.pbs.org/wgbh/buildingbig/

Society of Women Engineers: Educational Outreach
aspire.swe.org/

Walk Through a Hydroelectric Plant
fwee.org/nw-hydro-tours/walk-through-a-hydroelectric-project/

Women at Work Museum
www.womenatworkmuseum.org/envision-engineering.html

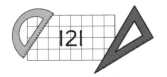